CRIME AND ENVIRONMENT

CROOM HELM SERIES IN GEOGRAPHY AND ENVIRONMENT

Edited by Alan Wilson, Nigel Thrift and Michael Bradford

A GEOGRAPHY OF THE LIFEWORLD
Movement, Rest and Encounter
DAVID SEAMON

CONCEPTS AND TECHNIQUES IN URBAN ANALYSIS
'BOLA AYENI

REGIONAL ECONOMIC PLANNING
Generation of Regional Input-Output Tables
R.C. JENSEN, T.D. MANDEVILLE AND N.D. KARUNARATNE

TRANSPORT NETWORK PLANNING
PATRICK O'SULLIVAN, GARY D. HOLTZCLAW AND GERALD BARBER

INFORMATION THEORY AND URBAN SPATIAL STRUCTURE
M.J. WEBBER

THE LARGE INDUSTRIAL ENTERPRISE
Some Spatial Perspectives
H.D. WATTS

REGIONS IN CRISIS
New Perspectives in European Regional Theory
EDITED BY JOHN CARNEY, RAY HUDSON AND JIM LEWIS

URBAN HOUSING PROVISION AND THE DEVELOPMENT PROCESS
DAVID DRAKAKIS-SMITH

URBAN TRANSPORT PLANNING
Theory and Practice
JOHN BLACK

HUMANISTIC GEOGRAPHY AND LITERATURE
Essays on the Experience of Place
DOUGLAS C.D. POCOCK

PLANNING IN THE SOVIET UNION
JUDITH PALLOT AND DENIS J.B. SHAW

CATASTROPHE THEORY AND BIFURCATION
Applications to Urban and Regional Systems
A.G. WILSON

THEMES IN GEOGRAPHIC THOUGHT
MILTON E. HARVEY AND BRIAN P. HOLLY

REGIONAL LANDSCAPES AND HUMANISTIC GEOGRAPHY
EDWARD RELPH

Crime and Environment

R.N. DAVIDSON

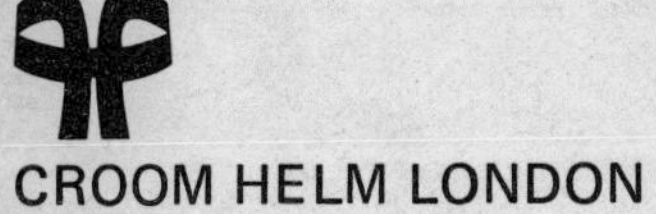

CROOM HELM LONDON

Croom Helm Ltd, 2-10 St John's Road, London SW11

British Library Cataloguing in Publication Data

Davidson, R.N.
Crime and environment. – (Croom Helm series in geography and environment)
1. Crime and criminals
2. Man – Influence of environment
I. Title
364'.042 HV6150

ISBN 0-7099-0803-2

Printed and bound in Great Britain
by Billing and Sons Limited
Guildford, London, Oxford, Worcester

CONTENTS

TABLES

FIGURES

for Val

ACKNOWLEDGEMENTS

No work of this length is produced without debts of gratitude. Colleagues, friends and family have all made room at times for my endeavours and I thank them for their forbearance. I am especially indebted to Professors Harry Wilkinson and Barry Johnston for the facilities and stimulus of their Departments at Hull and Canterbury Universities respectively. Hull University, moreover, allowed me study leave which provided much needed breathing space in the early stages of the project. My particular thanks are due to Mrs Sue Lightfoot for typing the final draft manuscript and to Joyce, Anna, Janet and others who variously typed earlier drafts. I wish also to acknowledge the material assistance of the Hull University Drawing Service in the preparation of illustrations, especially Keith Scurr but also Derek, Pat and Andrew.

Much of my interest in crime was kindled during a project, financially supported by the Social Science Research Council, on the analysis of urban sub-areas. I owe a particular debt to Keith Bottomley and Clive Coleman for allowing me to be associated with their research on criminal statistics, also supported by the SSRC, and to use their data. Both projects would not have been possible without the active support and assistance of the Hull, now Humberside, Police. I acknowledge a similar debt to the New Zealand Police, Christchurch District, for access to police records and the experience of seeing how they are compiled.

The following publishers are acknowledged for permission to use materials in which they hold the copyright: National Council for Geographic Education for Figures 1.1 and 1.4 reproduced from K.D. Harries, 'The Geography of American Crime, 1968', Figures 10 and 1 in *Journal of Geography* 70(4), 204-13, 1971; Oxford University Press and the Institute of Race Relations for Figures 1.5, 1.7 and 1.9 reproduced from J.R. Lambert, *Crime, Police and Race Relations*, 1970, Maps 11, 10 and 9; Association of American Geographers for Figure 1.8 reproduced from P.D. Phillips, 'Risk Related Crime Rates and Crime Patterns', Figure 1 in *Proceedings AAG*, 5, 201-4, 1973; John Baldwin, A.E. Bottoms and Tavistock Publications Ltd for Figures 2.1 and 2.3 reproduced from J. Baldwin and A.E. Bottoms, *The Urban Criminal*, 1976, Maps 3 and 4; and the New Zealand Geographical Society Inc.

for Figure 2.4 reproduced from R.N. Davidson, 'Patterns of Residential Burglary in Christchurch', Map 2 in *New Zealand Geographer* 36(2), 73-8, 1980.

INTRODUCTION

Interest in the geographical distribution of crime is over one hundred years old, dating back to the earliest collection of criminal statistics by Guerry in France. The interest of geographers in crime is rather more recent, hardly more than a couple of decades with one or two notable earlier exceptions. But such distinctions are invidious for as criminology has developed and broadened its base so has interest in the diverse ways in which environmental factors are implicated in crime. Geographers are not alone in commenting on these roles for, although they regard spatial distributions as their domain, other social scientists have not remained unaware of the importance of locating events. This is a book by a geographer but not exclusively for geographers.

Crime has risen dramatically in the last two decades in most Western countries. The problem of law and order is not a new issue in the political arena, but impetus has been given to the search for new and more sophisticated ways of dealing with crime in an age of fast-changing technology. As with crime itself, the resources to combat it are far from evenly distributed. The recurrent theme of this book is the extent and significance of spatial inequalities in patterns of crime and justice in their various guises, but it is not a theme dogmatically pursued to the exclusion of other relevancies.

The approach adopted to the definition of both crime and environment is decidedly eclectic. The problem with defining crime is that it is impossible to achieve an adequate generalisation to embrace all perspectives. Taking crime as events proscribed by the law is insufficient, as most infractions never receive the law's sanction. Limiting crime to events which fall within the sphere of operations of the criminal justice system likewise ignores the many that should but do not. Moreover, such definitions may have little to do with explaining criminal behaviour and its distribution in society, nor indeed with understanding responses to the general problem of crime and to becoming a victim. The works reviewed in this book encompass a variety of different definitions of crime: these will be made clear and the implications discussed where appropriate. Indeed, by comparing rather different approaches to the same problem, additional insights may often be gained. The major emphasis will be on crimes against the person and against property as these form the core of what is commonly identified and acknowledged as crime.

Similar problems exist with definitions of environment. Strictly speaking the environment consists of all phenomena perceived as exogenous to the individual. However, as psychological theories form a distinct realm within criminology and these emphasise the influence of socialisation and other processes within the tight bounds of kinship, the immediate or family environment is largely excluded from the discussion. Beyond the home, however, the environment is taken in all its aspects – as pure location, as a physical setting, as a social milieu, as a cultural realm or merely as a perceptual world. Nor will different meanings of environment be ignored for, as Taylor (1973) concludes, conceptualisation of the environment can be as important as its content. Environments can be seen as pure territory – a map for behaviour; or as something to be adapted or manipulated – an instrument in behaviour; or as something to be commandeered – a vehicle for behaviour. Environments also have scale. What is significant at the streetcorner may not be so for neighbourhood, city or region.

Traditional emphasis within criminology has been towards crimes and criminals as officially recorded: the orientation of Chapters 1 and 2 is towards disparities in the distribution of these. There are obvious limitations in studies based on official statistics – not least the observation that the bulk of crime never reaches the official record – an issue that is examined later in Chapter 4. Whether flawed or not the mainstream efforts to analyse crime rates need to be reviewed. Offences are discussed by types of crime and offenders according to their personal characteristics. No particular merit is seen in this scheme apart from the contrasts that emerge between categories in terms of inequalities at various scales.

Chapter 3 is directed towards a critical evaluation of the contribution of ecological dimensions to an understanding of disparities in crime rates. The ecological tradition is some fifty years old but has recently fallen into disrepute for several powerful reasons which are outlined. If all-embracing ecological theories are no longer tenable, there remain observable associations between the characteristics of areas and the nature and extent of crime suffered. These associations form the basis for a typology of urban neighbourhoods as criminal areas.

Focus is shifted to the victims of crime in Chapter 4. The relationship between real and official crime rates is evaluated – how are the official rates produced; are there disparities between areas in this process? The risks of victimisation are examined. Who are the victims? Does the place where the incident takes place have a bearing not just on who the victim is but also on the consequences of the act? Perceptions, fears and attitudes *vis-à-vis* crime also vary from area to area. Are they related to patterns of victimisation? How do neighbourhoods achieve a reputation as criminal areas? Much crime is highly localised and neighbourhoods act as a frame of reference for victims as well as offenders. Four alternative models of community responses to crime are postulated.

The distribution of justice is a further arena where widespread spatial inequalities are evident. Their scale and the extent to which they reflect legitimate concern with differences in the nature and seriousness of offences is the subject of Chapter 5. While the dispensation of justice is the formal prerogative of the courts, discretion is also exercised by other servants of the criminal justice system, notably the police, which has informal but nevertheless significant effects. Spatial bias in court discretion is illustrated by a case-study and the interactions between justice and the community are discussed.

In Chapter 6, the disparate material on offences, offenders and victims is integrated in a discussion of the various roles played by environmental factors in crime. These include scale and distance effects expressing the constraints on the behavioural world of individuals, whether offenders or victims; the environment as a source of opportunities which predispose some individuls to offend or which precipitate particular events; and the environment as an element in the labelling process whereby areas acquire reputations which circumscribe reponses to crime.

Formal conclusions are avoided in the final chapter. This does not imply that no useful lessons are to be learnt from the relations between crime and environment: indeed this is far from the case. But to translate understanding crime into policies for its control is to enter a completely new ball game. A new set of rules is required and the pitfalls of ignoring them are considerable. There is a growing movement to place more emphasis on environmental factors as a source of crime control policy (Clarke, 1980). My final comments reflect on the dangers and difficulties facing this movement not so much to deny its validity nor temper its optimism as to provide a sounder basis for evaluating the criteria for success. There is, moreover, some justification for the view that crime is here to stay and that more attention should be devoted to coping with it rather than controlling it.

My aim is to present evidence, to sift, sort and evaluate it, to examine the validity of assumptions and assess the merit of inferences drawn. The range of topics covered is wide and the treatment given to some of them is perforce limited. Methodologies are equally diverse, from high-powered statistical analyses to intimate observations of small-scale events. The reader will find no blockbusting theory of environment and crime because I do not believe there is one to be found. I am very much aware that environmental factors are but one element in wider explanations of crime, to which, from my narrow perspective, I may at times do rather less than full justice. If no simple answer is sought, the full flavour of the subtle and varied ways the environment is implicated in crime can stand revealed.

1 OFFENCES AND THE ENVIRONMENT

The Classification of Offences

The most important basic distinction to be made within the range of criminal acts is between offences against the person and those against property. The former will include the homicide group (murder, manslaughter, infanticide); assaults and woundings; sexual offences; and robbery. Property offences comprise various kinds of theft; trust offences such as fraud and embezzlement; criminal damage; and arson. A third category is less easily defined in strictly criminal terms – so-called social disorganisation offences including drunkenness, drug-taking and prostitution. Although this third group properly demands examination of its environmental correlates, data difficulties are quite severe, and the discussion will focus primarily on personal and property offences. These distinctions are complicated in Britain by the method of prosecuting offenders. The 1977 Criminal Law Act redefined modes of trial: offences labelled 'serious' in British criminal statistics refer to those which are tried (1) only on indictment at a Crown Court or (2) either on indictment or summarily at a magistrates' court at the discretion of the defendant. The scope of 'serious' offences differs slightly from the previous 'indictable' category (see Home Office, 1980, sections 1.17 and 1.18), but the terms will be used interchangeably in this volume. Most property offences are in the 'serious' category but a large number of minor assaults remain in the 'summary' category. Similar definitional problems exist in the United States with the FBI statistics.

Table 1.1 gives the breakdown of serious offences for England and Wales in 1979. The predominance of property offences is abundantly clear – over 95 per cent of the total. In terms of numbers, offences against the person are much rarer (about 5 per cent). In order to highlight right away some of the considerable variation which exists in the incidence of different types of offending, location quotients are calculated for three contrasting police authorities. The Metropolitan Police is by far the largest police force in Britain – some 22 per cent of serious crime in England and Wales occurs within its jurisdiction. Robbery is the offence which is relatively most prevalent in London. Sexual offences and violence are well below the national proportion.

Humberside is a medium-sized county, fairly urbanised but with-

Table 1.1: Serious Offences Recorded as Known to the Police: England and Wales, 1979

	England and Wales No.	%	Location quotients[a] London[b]	Humberside	Lincolnshire
Violence against the person	94,960	3.7	77	147	133
Sexual offences	21,843	0.9	57	149	202
Robbery	12,482	0.5	226	43	29
Burglary	549,138	21.6	98	105	87
Theft and handling stolen goods	1,416,143	55.8	102	94	101
Fraud and forgery	118,033	4.6	100	54	85
Criminal damage	320,469	12.6	100	119	109
Other offences	3,669	0.1	66	79	201
				No. of offences	
Total	2,536,737	100.0[c]	564,187	48,195	17,539

a. Location quotients measure the concentration of serious offences relative to the national average. An area with exactly the national average proportion of offences in a category would have an LQ of 100 for that category. The higher the LQ, the greater the proportionate incidence of that offence type.
b. Metropolitan Police District and City of London.
c. Percentage column does not add up due to rounding.
Source: Home Office (1980), Table 32; LQ calculations by author.

out a large conurbation. It stands in marked contrast to London, with a high proportionate incidence of personal violence and sexual offences and lower than average rates for robbery and fraud. The patterns for Lincolnshire, a largely rural police area, present yet further contrasts. While sexual offences occupy a higher proportion than in either of the more urbanised areas, personal violence is not so exaggerated as in Humberside. As might be expected, robbery is least likely in the rural context although, curiously, criminal damage is relatively more prevalent. Burglary is less common in Lincolnshire but otherwise it and theft show little tendency to be differentiated between police areas.

The lesson to be learnt from these figures is that any breakdown of the crime rates, either by areas or by types of crime, instantly reveals considerable and conflicting disparities. And this is only within officially recorded crime: true crime rates may be of the order of two to ten times higher. Moreover, the relationship between true and official crime is itself subject to wide variation. In America, victimisation surveys have found (Table 1.2) that only 27 per cent of rape incidents get reported and the proportion of burglaries notified to the police is little higher. At the other extreme, for homicide and vehicle theft, reported crime

Table 1.2: Relations Between Real and Official Crime Rates: United States, 1965-6

Crime type	Rates per 100,000 population		Official as per cent of real
	Real[a]	Official[b]	
Homicide	3.0	5.1	170
Forcible rape	42.5	11.6	27
Robbery	94.0	61.4	65
Aggravated assault	218.3	106.6	49
Burglary	949.1	296.6	31
Larceny (over $50)	606.5	267.4	44
Vehicle theft	206.2	226.0	110
All Part I Crimes	2119.6	974.7	46

a. Estimated from national victimisation survey.
b. Uniform crime reports adjusted to exclude non-residential burglary and larceny.
Source: Ennis (1967).

actually exceeds estimates of the true incidence (homicide victims don't normally have the opportunity of reporting their experience; insurance considerations motivate reporting vehicle theft). Overall rather less than half of serious crime in the United States is reported. In a survey of London, Sparks *et al.* (1977) suggest that less than one-third of criminal victimisations are notified to the police. From the official rate we cannot tell whether the high proportion of sexual offences in Lincolnshire is because that county is a hotbed of sexual deviation or because such offences are much more likely to be reported in tightknit rural and small town communities.

Gross Offence Rate

International comparisons of gross offence rates are almost impossible because of differences in the scope and coverage of legal and judicial systems. At various sub-national spatial scales, however, the gross rate provides an introduction to the discussion of particular crimes. Even so we should be wise not to expect too much from the gross offence rate – it can, as we shall see, be quite misleading.

(a) Regional Variations

Regional variations in overall crime rates can be considerable. Harries (1971), in a study of the United States, shows that the rate varies from 634 offences per 100,000 population (North Dakota) to 3,764 (California). In general, crime rates are highest in the most urbanised regions (Northeast, Midwest and Pacific coast) and lowest in the rural Mountain, Great Plains and Southern states (see Figure 1.1). In Britain

Figure 1.1: Regional Variation in Gross Crime Rate: United States, 1968

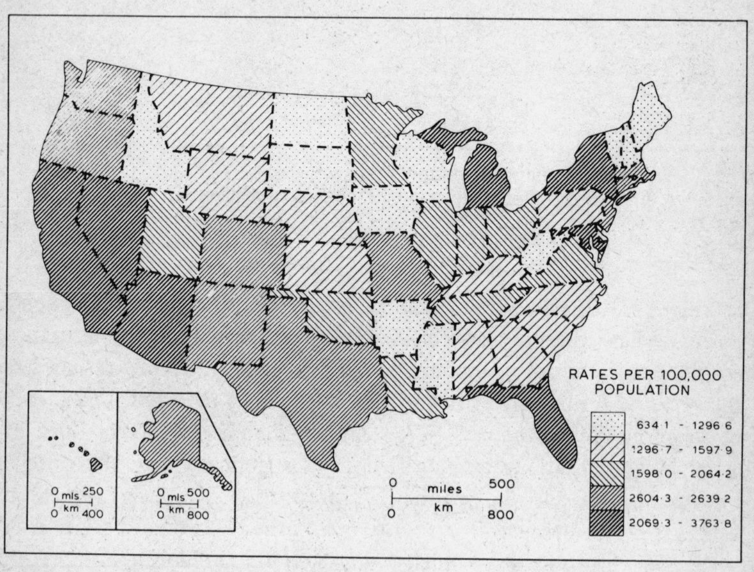

Source: Harries (1971), Figure 10.

regional variations are less exaggerated but nevertheless are still clear (Figure 1.2). However, most commentators on this level of analysis take pains to point out that, with the exception of violence, the real relationship is between crime and urbanisation and that regional variations coincidentally reflect differences between regions in the size and importance of urban agglomerations.

(b) Inter-urban Variations

The most significant observation to be made at this level is that the crime rate increases with city size. Larger cities have more than their fair share of criminal activity. In Britain, London's crime rate is only slightly higher than that of the next six largest cities (Table 1.3) but these in turn have twice as much crime as the smallest rural counties. In the

Figure 1.2: Regional Variation in Gross Crime Rate: England and Wales, 1979

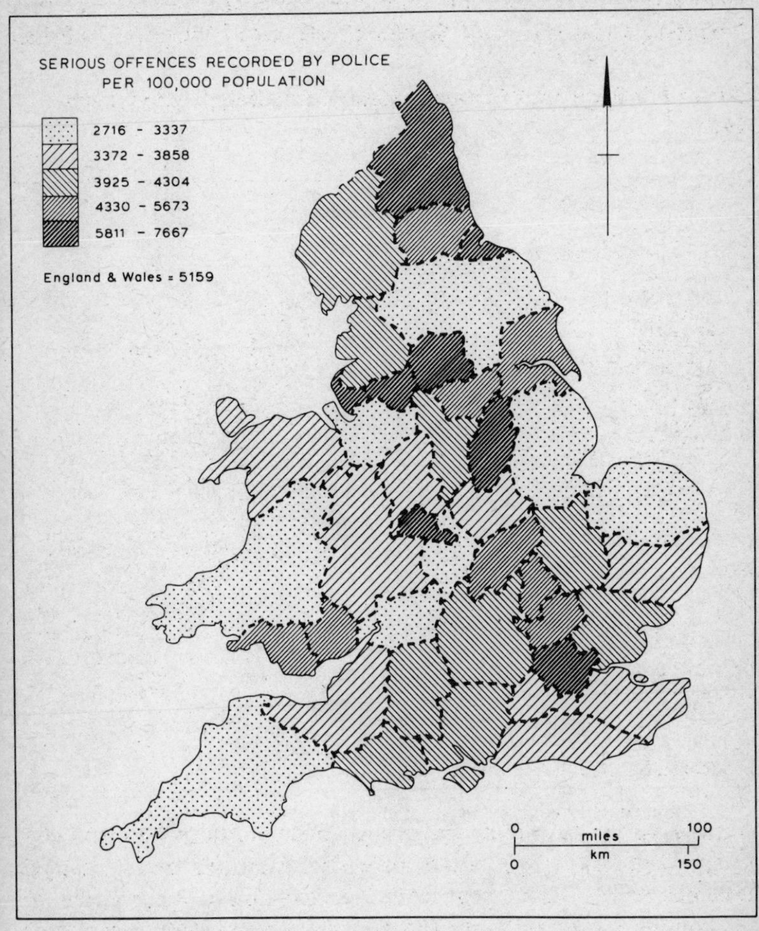

Source: Compiled by author from Home Office (1980), Table 2.14.

United States a similar pattern exists (Table 1.4). The size of the country perhaps exaggerates the smoothness of the trend, and the extent of disparities between the largest and smallest cities may be widened by the American organisation of police jurisdictions which tends to separate suburban areas from the city proper. Nevertheless, it is clear that crime is primarily an urban phenomenon.

Apart from size, other characteristics have been related to the

Table 1.3: Crime Rates for Selected Major Crimes: England and Wales, 1965

Type of police area	Reported crimes per 100,000 total population: Offences against the person	Breaking offences and robbery	Larcenies	All indictable
London	9	434	1122	3378
6 very large towns	17	473	646	3327
11 large towns	9	358	499	3333
29 medium-sized towns	5	302	434	2795
27 small towns	5	229	350	2544
6 very large counties	4	244	311	1835
17 large counties	4	195	298	1670
17 medium-sized counties	5	176	289	1770
10 small counties	5	147	266	1719

Source: McClintock and Avison (1968), Tables 3.5 and 3.10.

Table 1.4: Crime Rates and City Size: United States, 1965

City size	Reported crimes per 100,000 total population: Violence[a]	Property[b]	All serious crimes[c]
over 1 million	503	2250	2753
500,000-1 million	377	2204	2581
250,000-500,000	286	2063	2349
100,000-250,000	241	1780	2021
50,000-100,000	146	1464	1610
25,000- 50,000	113	1217	1330
10,000- 25,000	94	912	1006
under 10,000	81	704	785
suburban areas	107	1064	1171
rural areas	81	535	616

a. Homicide, rape, robbery, aggravated assault.
b. Burglary, larceny (over $50), auto theft.
c. FBI Index crimes, i.e. a plus b.
Source: FBI, *Uniform Crime Reports.*

crime rate. One which has caused much furious debate is population density. One argument has it that higher densities lead to greater stress and therefore to increased crime. This pathological process is supported by empirical observation that larger cities do indeed tend to have higher densities and by experimental evidence from animal populations that crowding leads to deviant behaviour. In contradiction, it has been noted that a consistent rise in urban crime rates this century has been matched by an equally consistent fall in densities. The connection between crime and density is far from simple: we will return to it later.

Many demographic and social characteristics of cities are related to their crime rates. In many cases the relationship is coincidental – a product of the fact that criminal activity is more common in certain types and classes of people. For instance, since young people are more likely to offend than older, it follows that growing cities (which have a youthful population) are likely to have a higher crime rate, irrespective of other factors. A similar situation arises with social class, economic status and (in America particularly) ethnic origin.

Harries (1974), in his analysis of the 134 largest metropolitan areas in the United States, identifies a 'general crime' factor with which most types of offence with the exception of homicide and assault are related. This factor is associated with seven socio-economic indices. Thus cities with a high crime rate tend to have (1) larger populations; (2) fewer jobs in manufacturing; (3) higher *per capita* incomes; (4) greater social disorganisation (e.g. divorce); (5) higher rates of population change; (6) more unemployment; and (7) larger black population. Harries concludes that this is some sort of opportunity factor which he contrasts with a rather different violent crime factor.

(c) Variations Within Cities

The most striking feature of the general distribution of crime within cities is its concentration in the centre and diminishing incidence towards the periphery. Figures for Sheffield illustrate this pattern (Table 1.5): 38 per cent of offences occurred within one mile of the city centre. However, this neat concentric arrangement should be viewed with some caution. As we shall see, the distribution of particular types of offence may diverge markedly from the general model. Likewise, the aggregation of crimes into statistical sub-divisions of the city

Table 1.5: Location of Offences in Relation to Distance From City Centre: Sheffield, 1966

All offences (indictable)	Number	%
Within ½ mile of city centre	2616	23.7
½-1 mile from centre	1580	14.3
1-3 miles from centre	5624	50.9
over 3 miles from centre	1233	11.1
location not known	258	–
Total	11,311	100.0

Source: Baldwin and Bottoms (1976), Table 4.

(wards, census tracts, etc.) in order to calculate the rate tends to conceal localised variations. There have as a consequence been few successful analyses of the gross offence rates in cities except in a most superficial manner. The separation of personal and property crimes is at least necessary.

Notwithstanding these limitations, it should be noted that variations in the incidence of offences *within* cities are greater than *between* cities. As Figure 1.3 indicates, even in a medium-sized English city

Figure 1.3: Location of Indictable Offences: Hull, 1972

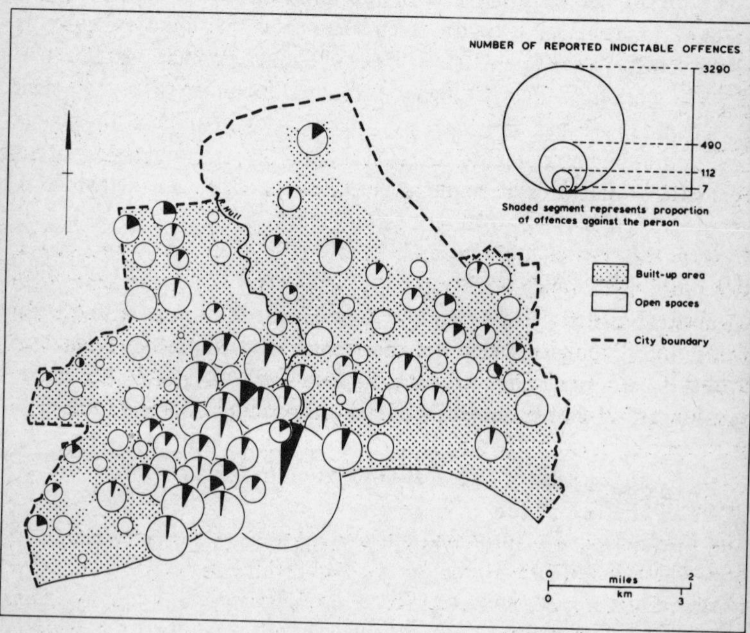

Source: Author's survey (figures grossed up from 1 in 7 sample).

not noted for its criminality, the number of offences in areas of about 3,000 population ranges from practically nil to nearly 500, even when the city centre (where over 3,200 offences were committed) is excluded. The tendency for crime to diminish from the centre is evidently no more than a general rule and there are many anomalies to it.

Offences Against the Person

Any discussion of the location of crimes of violence must recognise one important fact. Many victims are not attacked by the stranger of popular myth. Table 1.6 gives some comparative figures for 17 US cities.

Table 1.6: Relationship Between Offender and Victim: 17 US Cities, 1967

Relationship	Criminal homicide	Aggravated assault	Forcible rape	Robbery	All crimes of violence
	Percentages				
Family	24.7	13.9	6.9	0.6	11.1
Friend or acquaintance	37.1	31.0	35.9	11.8	27.7
Stranger	17.3	30.8	53.1	82.2	45.8
Unknown	20.9	24.3	4.1	5.4	15.4
Total	100.0	100.0	100.0	100.0	100.0

Source: Mulvihill and Tumin (1969), adapted from Table 6.

Only in the case of robbery, with 82 per cent of attacks by strangers, does the myth hold. With rape the proportion is 53 per cent, with aggravated assault 31 per cent and homicide 17 per cent. With the exception of robbery where the proportion is much lower, friends and acquaintances (including neighbours, etc.) are responsible for about one-third of crimes of violence. These differences reinforce the need to treat each crime as a separate entity.

(a) Murder

The homicide group, of which murder is the dominant constituent, is one where spatial variations are perhaps least significant among all types of crime. At all scales of analysis, regional, urban or local, murders tend to be less concentrated in particular areas. This reflects the position of murder as a crime of passion, focusing on interpersonal relations and normally paying scant regard to external environmental conditions. In Britain this situation is more evident than in the United States (Table 1.7) – the lower murder rate reflecting, among other things, a lower incidence of premeditated or coincidental slayings. Note, however, that murder in Britain is slowly becoming a more impersonal crime (Home Office, 1980, Table 10.3). The micro-locations of murder are moreover less differentiated than other crimes of violence (Table 1.8). Although indoor locations are in the majority (60 per cent) and the home is most popular (34 per cent) the concentration in the

Table 1.7: Victims of Homicide: England and Wales, 1967 and 1976

Relationship with suspect	Percentages 1967	1976
Relative (incl. spouse, cohabitant)	53	40
Other acquaintance, associate	30	33
Stranger	10	18
Not known	7	9
Total	100	100

Source: Criminal Statistics, England and Wales, 1976, Table 8.4.

Table 1.8: Micro-location of Crimes of Violence: 17 US Cities, 1967

Location	Criminal homicide	Aggravated assault	Percentages Forcible rape	Robbery	All crimes of violence
In the house	34.3	26.3	51.5	11.3	27.8
Elsewhere indoors	26.2	19.3	13.9	21.7	20.3
In the street	24.9	39.1	4.8	43.1	32.1
Elsewhere outside	12.0	13.0	29.1	23.7	18.3
Unknown	2.5	2.2	0.7	0.2	1.5
Total	100.0	100.0	100.0	100.0	100.0

Note: Columns may not add up due to rounding.
Source: Mulvihill and Tumin (1969), adapted from Table 7.

most common location is not comparatively strong. However, murders are localised in the sense that they frequently occur in proximity to the suspect's residence, if not actually there: 66 per cent of murders in Akron, Ohio took place in the same census tract as lived arrested suspects (Pyle, 1976a).

There is one scale of analysis where variations in murder rates begin to emerge as significant. This is the regional scale. In Britain, it has been noted that Scotland has a rather higher incidence of murder (and other violent crimes) but the overall rarity of murder has made reliable conclusions rather difficult. In America, this has been less of a problem and the higher murder rates of the Deep South have received a certain amount of attention. Early geographical attempts to explain this phenomenon relied on simple physical determinism. Ellsworth Huntington (1945) related the high murder rate to summer heat. More recently, Gastil (1971) proposed an explanation based on the theory of a regional culture of violence – that Southerners have, by tradition, more entrenched patterns of violent behaviour, easier access to weapons and a higher tolerance to violent acts, especially by whites towards blacks. Subsequent critics (Loftin and Hill, 1974; Doerner, 1975), while not denying that murder rates in the South are generally higher (Figure 1.4), have pointed out that the region and its culture are less

Figure 1.4: Regional Distribution of Homicide: United States, 1968

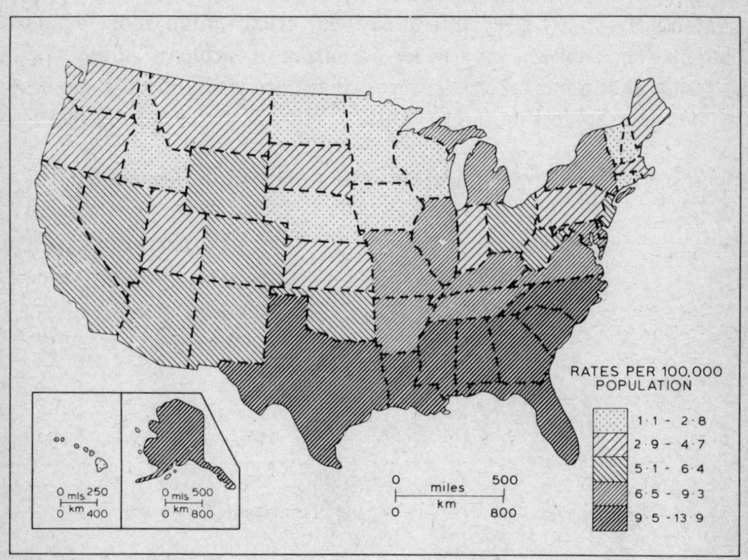

Source: Harries (1971), Figure 1.

easily defined than Gastil suggests. There has, moreover, been a convergence in recent decades between Southern rates and those of other regions and there remain, unexplained by the theory, variations between states (and smaller areas) within the South.

(b) Assault

Assaults form numerically the largest sub-group of offences against the person. McClintock (1963) in a study of London suggests that important differences are highlighted by classifying assaults on the basis of the situation of the offence. He distinguishes six types:

(1) attacks in order to perpetrate a sexual offence (6 per cent of the total);
(2) attacks on police officers, civilians intervening or weapons offences (12 per cent);

(3) domestic and neighbourhood disputes (31 per cent);
(4) fights in pubs, etc. (20 per cent);
(5) violence in public places (30 per cent);
(6) a residual, other circumstances category (1 per cent).

Assaults do very clearly tend to occur in particular places.

Lambert (1970) gives this situational classification more detailed examination. Drawing on a wider definition of incidents (those where no police action was taken), he shows that disputes in Birmingham have distinct geographical patterns (Figure 1.5) – 67 per cent took place in

Figure 1.5: Approximate Location of Minor Disputes: Birmingham, 1966-7

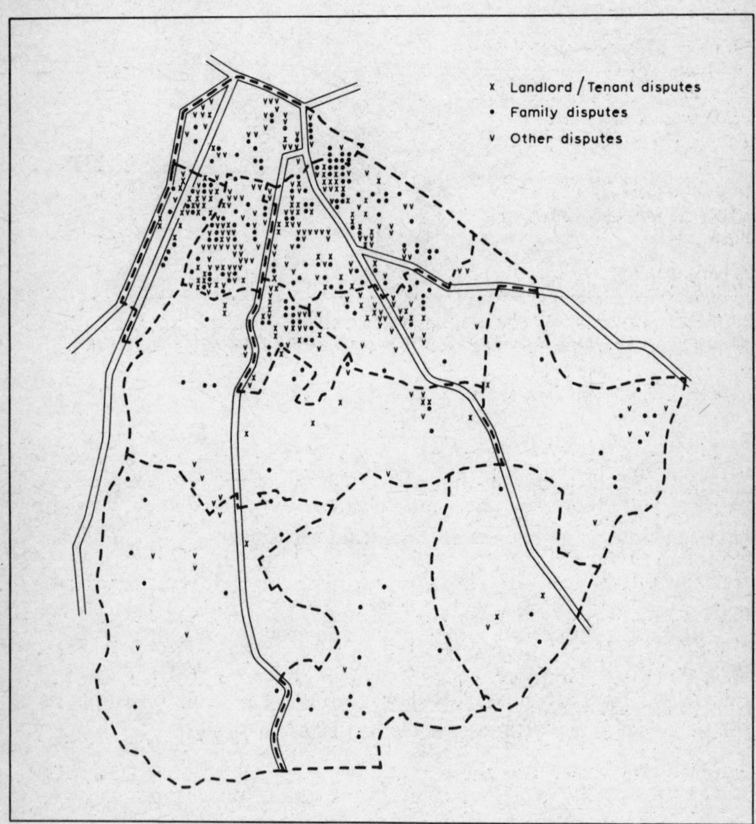

Source: Lambert (1970), Map 11. ©IRR, 1970.

the older, decaying inner-city parts of his survey area where about one-third of its population lived. The outer, more modern suburban areas held 44 per cent of the population but only 11 per cent of disputes. McClintock (1963) reports a similar distribution for London – a concentration on the ring of seedy, run-down areas which surround the central business district. These areas have poor housing and frequently a high turnover of population. They often contain a concentration of pubs and clubs which have not been dispersed to the periphery as fast as population under urban renewal.

Table 1.9: Minor Disputes: Birmingham, 1966-7

Type of dispute	No. of incidents	%	Index of geographical concentration[a]
Between tenants and landlords (or their agents)	97	17	49.2
Between tenants in same house or between neighbours	75	13	32.4
Between members of the same family	224	40	31.7
In public places	99	18	51.6
Other (in shops, at work, on buses, etc.)	65	12	40.1
All disputes	560	100	38.9

a. This will be zero if the geographical distribution is identical to that of the population as a whole; it would be 100 if all disputes were in one of the ten districts in the sector.
Source: Lambert (1970), derived from data given in Table 19.

Further analysis of Lambert's figures (Table 1.9) reveals that there are marked locational differences between the various types of dispute. The most numerous, family disputes (40 per cent of the total), are least geographically concentrated: more common in the middle and outer zones; 68 per cent of disputes on peripheral council estates were between members of the same family and the percentage was also above average in the part of the inner-city where council flats had replaced older property. In many ways this is the type of dispute closest in distributional characteristics to murder. Disputes between tenants or neighbours are also more evenly distributed than the average, with the middle zone, especially those parts where there is sub-division of big, old houses, having a greater incidence of this type. On the other hand, areas of council housing, both inner-city and peripheral, tend to have fewer of these disputes. Incidents between landlords and tenants are, as might be expected, highly concentrated in the parts of the inner-city where private rented accommodation is most common. Disputes in public places are more frequent in the inner-city where such places are located or frequented. The remainder are not sufficiently numerous to allow disaggregation. If they were, quite specific locational emphasis would emerge since we know that shops, workplaces, etc. are not evenly distributed throughout the city. It is perhaps worth noting the situational ties involved in many disputes: the disputants are frequently tied by kinship, residential proximity or contractual obligations.

In North America, the incidence of assault, as with other crimes of violence, is rather higher and the emphasis is towards more impersonal, street crimes. Yet beyond this the patterns are not dissimilar. As with murder, there are distinct micro-locational attributes (Table 1.8). Unlike murder, at the neighbourhood level, particular environments begin to emerge where incidents are concentrated. At the inter-urban level we find that assault shows a smaller increase in rate with city size than murder (see Figure 1.6).

Figure 1.6: City Size and Violent Crime Rates: United States, 1978

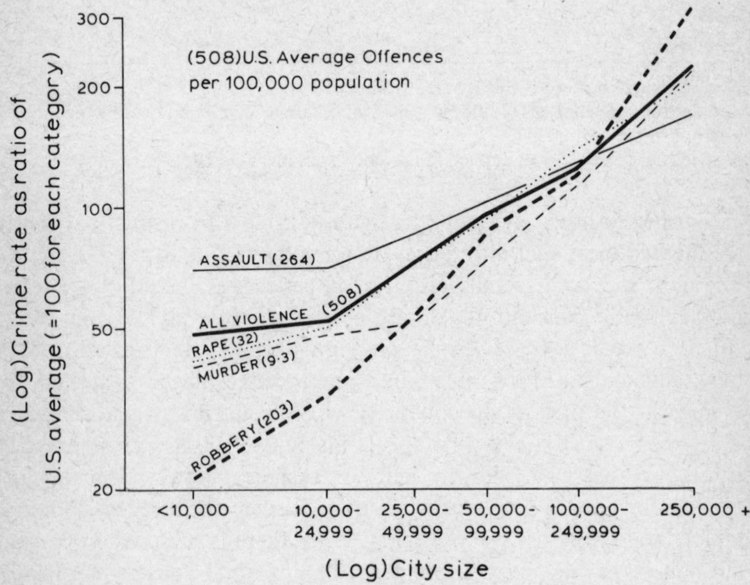

Source: FBI, *Uniform Crime Reports* (1978).

(c) Rape

Rape is sufficiently rare in Britain to preclude reliable locational studies, though there is an accumulation of case-history evidence to suggest that spatial concentrations exist and that there are significant environmental factors, broadly in line with more detailed North American studies. The most thorough of these is Amir's (1971) work on rape in Philadelphia. He concludes that many of the myths surrounding this offence are unjustified. Most rapes (71 per cent) are planned and 48 per cent of victims were previously acquainted with the offender (14 per cent intimately). In Philadelphia, 56 per cent of rapes took place in one of the participant's homes (cf. Table 1.8 which refers to the average for 17 US cities). The commonest outdoor location is a motor vehicle. As may be expected rape is rare in public spaces. Amir also indicates that there is a strong neighbourhood link in rape cases. In 73 per cent of cases victim and offender live in the same neighbourhood and in 68 per cent the offence took place there also. There is, moreover, a tendency for victim and offender to be of the same race and age-group. The indication is that rape, despite micro-locational similarities to murder, is more like assault in its environmental correlates, being associated most closely with poorer inner-city areas. At the macro-scale the incidence of rape rises more rapidly with city size than assault though not as dramatically (in relation to the average rate) as robbery (Figure 1.6).

(d) Other Sex Offences

Since there are considerable national divergencies over the definition of many other sexual crimes, and in many cases there have been several changes of attitude and statute in recent years, this section will be mainly restricted to the area where there is some degree of unanimity – sex offences against juveniles. These in fact constitute the majority of victims – 84.5 per cent in Britain (Radzinowicz, 1957). Included here are unlawful sexual intercourse (USI), pederasty and other forms of child molesting, incest, and some other rarer offences. Again the incidence is low and this type of offence has received little attention. What evidence there is suggests that incest, certainly, is more common among the inhabitants of poorer districts. The proportion reported is probably very low and it may well be more prevalent in other environments than the official cases indicate. Likewise, unlawful sexual intercourse may be reported relatively infrequently and in circumstances which promote bias. Usually cases come forward at the insistence of a parent. Sometimes the police will refuse to take action if there is evidence of previous sexual experience on the part of the girl. Biased or not the majority of incidents reported are in inner-city areas. Child molesting contrasts with patterns for USI and incest in many ways. It is likely to be perpetrated by a stranger (Walmsley and White, 1979) and in a public place (though the role of neighbours should not be discounted). It is more widespread throughout the city though in micro-locational terms it may be concentrated where children congregate, e.g. parks, playgrounds, shops, etc.

At the wider scale, Radzinowicz (1957) shows that the rate of homosexual offending diminishes with city size in England and Wales. This finding, contrary to the trend of virtually all other offences, may be related to more relaxed attitudes in big cities at a time when the societal view of homosexuals was undergoing fairly rapid change. The comparative trend for heterosexual offences is less clearcut: large cities (excluding London) and rural areas have the highest rates whereas medium-sized cities are lower and London lowest of all. Regional variations are marked but without apparent logic. Yorkshire has the highest rate for heterosexual offences, but is below average for homosexual offences. The Southwest and Wales have the highest incidence of homosexual offending.

(e) Robbery

Robbery stands in contrast to other crimes of violence in many ways. It is the offence which above all has been associated in the public mind with the 'crime wave' and is therefore the prime target of the law and order lobby (a distinction it perhaps shares with vandalism). As a consequence it has been much studied and a wealth of information exists about its locational correlates. The primary contrasts with other crimes of violence are that it is committed largely by strangers (82 per cent on average for 17 US cities, Table 1.6) and more often outside (67 per cent, Table 1.8). Yet these figures baldly conceal considerable differences within the robbery classification. McClintock and Gibson (1961) use the location of the offence together with the type of victim to derive a classification of robberies into five main situational types. The proportions of each type from their London study are given in Table 1.10 together with Normandeau's (1969) parallel data for Philadelphia.

Robbery of employees (typically payroll robbery) is the dominant type in London and is increasing. Locationally this kind of robbery is dependent on the distribution of targets, so it tends to be concentrated in city centres and commercial or industrial districts. In contrast,

Table 1.10: Types of Robbery: McClintock and Gibson's Situational Classification

Type of robbery	Percentage of all robberies London (av. 1950, 1957, 1960)	Philadelphia (av. 1960-6)
1. Robbery of employees	41	26
2. Robbery in open following sudden attack (i.e. mugging)	33	52
3. Robbery on private premises	11	7
4. Robbery after preliminary association of short duration (mainly for sexual purposes)	12	10
5. Robbery of associate of some duration	4	5
Total	100	100

Note: Columns may not add up due to rounding.
Source: Normandeau (1969).

mugging is the main category in Philadelphia and is increasing there too, so the two cities continue to draw apart in the pattern of robberies. Mugging is also target orientated, but since the target is an individual, it is more prevalent in residential districts.

Typically, muggings are perpetrated by young males on older males (contrary to the myth of granny-bashing) and there is (commonly in America, increasing in Britain) a racial element in the attack. Since, as with many young offenders, muggers do not mug far from home, many of their victims come from the same sort of neighbourhood. Thus muggings tend to be concentrated in poorer, inner-city districts, especially those with a mixture of house-types, age or racial groups, or land uses. It is rather less common in the more traditional working-class area, but can be a problem in modern high-density housing developments. At the micro-scale three locational factors are important:

(1) the locus should be busy (and thus offer a good chance of a reasonable target) but not too busy (so that the attack is witnessed or interrupted). There is some evidence that *very* busy places are also popular since (and muggers are aware of this) potential helpers are immobilised or confused by the crowd situation (Conklin, 1975). A typical locus would be a street leading off a main thoroughfare or shopping centre. Quiet residential backwaters are rarely the scene of muggings.

(2) the locus should offer good opportunities for concealment, for example by being badly lit or with trees, shrubberies, etc.

(3) the locus should offer good opportunities for escape, for example alleyways, passages through buildings, etc.

The mugger will further benefit from having a good working knowledge of the distribution of these opportunities, thus reinforcing the premium on offending within his neighbourhood or at least close to it.

The remaining robbery groups are much less important. Robbery on private premises is usually residential robbery. Muggers and residential robbers share many characteristics, in age, motivation, etc., and share a lack of concern for contact with the victim (Reppetto, 1974). The main differences are in the target and perhaps most significantly in the time of day. Residential robberies peak in the late afternoon, muggings in the late evening. These two offences offer alternatives for criminal activity distinguished only by the fact that houses provide greater concealment during daylight hours when mugging is riskier. Residential robberies tend to be located in the same areas of cities as muggings though the distribution within cities may be more evenly spread. It is interesting to contrast these two crimes with residential burglary discussed below.

One final distributional feature of robbery should be emphasised. More than any other violent crime its incidence increases with city size (Figure 1.6). A clue to the high robbery rates in big cities may be in the importance of anonymity between offender and victim. Big cities are often characterised by greater anonymity in interpersonal relations of all kinds and the scale of neighbourhoods which provide the base for much criminal activity is much larger. However, we jump ahead.

Offences Against Property

We noted earlier (Table 1.1) that offences against property constitute the vast majority of serious crimes in England and Wales (and of serious crime in the United States: Table 1.2). Even taking a wider definition, theft of one kind or another still predominates. For example, Lambert (1970) in his study of a Birmingham police division reports that thefts accounted for 64 per cent of all events recorded by the police (including non-indictable offences and minor incidents but excluding traffic offences). So we are dealing here with a large and diverse group of offences. There are, moreover, within this group some fairly serious classification problems which should be noted before discussing the various categories of property offence.

Some of the problems are highlighted by a comparison of the breakdown of burglary and theft offences in Hull and the part of Birmingham studied by Lambert (1970). The most glaring discrepancies (Table 1.11) emerge in three areas: (1) residential burglary and theft; (2) non-

Table 1.11: A Comparison of Theft and Burglary in Hull and Birmingham

	Percentages			
	Hull[a]		Birmingham[b]	
Burglary				
Residential	21		5	
Non-residential	14		10	
Sub-total		35		15
Theft				
From a house	1		16	
From a meter	7		11	
Shoplifting	11		2	
Of a motor vehicle	3		3	
From an unattended motor vehicle	6		20	
Of a cycle	11		5	
Other thefts	25		29	
Sub-total		65		85
Total	100		100	
Percentage of thefts involving less than £10		57		61

a. From a random sample of all offences in 1972: author's survey.
b. From a sample taken in 'F' Division, Nov. 1966-Feb. 1967: Lambert (1970), Tables 9 and 12.
Note: In both cases, reported offences written off as 'no crime' are excluded. Columns may not add up due to rounding.

residential burglary and shoplifting; and (3) vehicle and cycle theft. While the definitions of burglary and theft were amended by the 1968 Theft Act which comes between the two survey dates, the categories in the table are not directly affected. What is affected is the interpretation of the definition of the various residential offences, particularly the many of a very petty nature. Thus a relaxation of the rule on what constitutes 'forced entry' (which results in a classification of burglary) may explain why Hull appears to have more burglaries and Birmingham more theft from a house. Theft from a meter is also problematic. In Hull, breaking open a gas or electricity meter is normally classified as burglary if the meter is situated in a dwelling to which entry has been forced. Meter thefts therefore tend to be restricted to situations where a door or window is left open, where the meter is accessible to the public (lodging houses, flats, but also some council houses for ease of meter reading) or where the occupant is the offender. This distinction is not consistently applied. So police practices can vary within a single authority as they most certainly do between authorities. By adding the three residential categories (29 per cent in Hull, 32 per cent in Birmingham) the differences are largely removed. This amalgamation will be adopted below, though it should be noted that many studies have treated the residential categories independently.

The disparities in the percentages for non-residential burglary and shoplifting are almost certainly due to the fact that Birmingham's central area is in another police division. Opportunities for these two offence groups are therefore more restricted in the area for which Lambert derived his data than in Hull where the figures refer to the whole city. The third and final group of discrepancies is again related to differences in the two places, but this time in terms of socio-economic variables. Income levels and car-ownership are higher in Birmingham and this must reflect in greater opportunities for vehicle theft. Hull has lower car-ownership and one of the highest rates of cycle use in Britain.

While these observations may make us somewhat more cautious in evaluating comparative rates of property crime than we were with violent crime there are, nevertheless, general trends in the distribution and incidence of this offence group. In both the United States and Britain there is a tendency for property crimes to increase with city size (see Tables 1.3 and 1.4). While the scope and content of these tables is quite different (many indictable larcenies in Britain, e.g. shoplifting, would not be classified as 'Index Crime' in the US), it is remarkable that the differentials between large and small cities in both countries are of the same order. It is surprising that any trend occurs when the widespread divergences in geographical distribution within cities are observed.

(a) Residential Theft

This group includes residential burglary, theft from or around dwellings and from prepayment meters. While many studies have treated these categories separately, there are sufficient distributional similarities to warrant regarding them as a homogeneous group. Lambert (1970) is one author who does exactly this and his map of the distribution of residential theft in a sector of Birmingham (Figure 1.7) serves as an introduction to this offence group. Some 61 per cent of house thefts in his sector occur in the inner zone giving a rate of 55 per 10,000 popula-

Figure 1.7: Approximate Location of Residential Theft: Birmingham, 1966-7

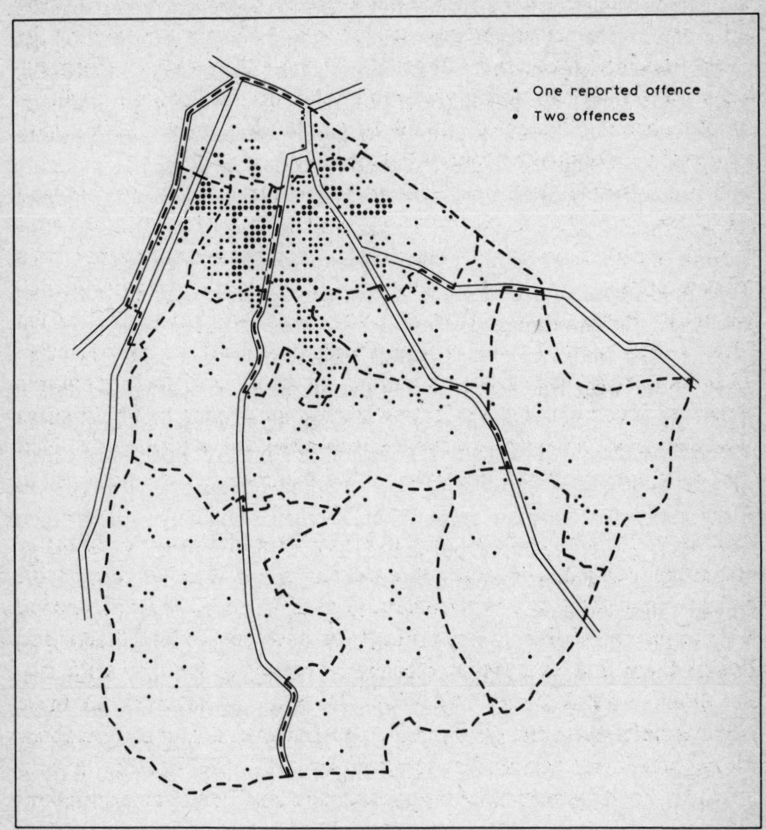

Source: Lambert (1970), Map 10. ©IRR, 1970.

tion. The middle zone contains 24 per cent with a rate of 31, and the outer zone 15 per cent with a rate of six. So these thefts are marginally less concentrated in the inner-city than the disputes we examined earlier but it is still a very uneven distribution. Within each zone there are further variations. Of the ten districts, the peak rate of 80 occurs in Balshall Heath which Lambert describes as an inner-city area of older housing much of which is scheduled for redevelopment. It has substantial coloured and Irish-born minorities. At the other end of the scale is Hall Green (four house thefts per 10,000 population) – an area on the fringe of the city consisting predominantly of modern semi-detached, owner-occupied houses.

In a study of Boston, Massachusetts, Reppetto (1974) indicates a similar basic pattern for residential burglaries. High rates occur in the core and adjacent districts and there is a rapid decline into the outlying areas. He also shows that, as in Birmingham, rates vary considerably within the rings: the incidence of burglary can show very localised concentrations. One factor found to be highly related to the neighbourhood burglary rate is the degree of social cohesion. Reppetto measured this on a three-point scale: (1) willingness to help others; (2) readiness to ask others to help; and (3) length of residence. Areas with a low degree of social cohesion in Boston tend to have a high burglary rate. Another factor of importance is the physical security of dwellings. Single family dwellings are less likely to be burgled than apartment blocks. Apartment blocks with restricted access (e.g. a porter) are safer than those with free access. Using these criteria Reppetto was able to rank the urban neighbourhoods of Boston. The lowest risk of burglary occurs in areas with high social cohesion or a high proportion of access-secure buildings, regardless of race, income or location. Next lowest risks apply to suburban or peripheral areas among which the affluent are likely to suffer more burglaries. The highest risks of burglary are reserved for inner-city areas where vulnerability rather than affluence is the key discriminant.

Vulnerability is essentially observed at the micro-locational level. What makes a burglar choose one house rather than another? To understand this we need to know something about burglars and their behaviour. The typical burglar, in both Britain and America, is a young male, usually aged between 15 and 20. Youthfulness is important. As Reppetto concludes, young burglars are more opportunist and less likely to plan their attacks. Opportunism leads to a number of (sometimes conflicting) situational criteria. The young burglar is more likely to offend in proximity to his residence or other places where he legitimately spends much of his time (e.g. workplace or pub): but this is where he is most likely to be recognised. He is more likely to take risks: but also to end up stealing very little. His target is therefore likely to be an unoccupied house in a rather poor district. Given a choice of targets, the opportunist burglar will select one that offers ease of access (unsecure doors, windows) and avoidance from observation (poor street-lighting, not overlooked). In Sheffield (Baldwin and Bottoms, 1976), 54 per cent of breaking offences occurred within one mile of the offender's residence (76 per cent of those committed by 10-15 year olds). In 91 per cent of all thefts within this distance less than £25-

worth of property was stolen. In Christchurch, New Zealand, a survey of burglary (Davidson, 1980b) revealed that of 86 Census Districts, the five richest (in terms of median male incomes in 1976) suffered six burglaries involving a loss of $1,204 whereas the five poorest districts had 46 burglaries with a loss of $7,044. The five most victimised districts suffered 161 burglaries in which $30,876 was stolen. Thirty-two per cent of burglaries (and 30 per cent of known burglars) were located in a small, compact area which from its socio-economic characteristics might be identified as Christchurch's 'zone-in-transition', and in which lived not quite 10 per cent of its population (see Figure 2.4 and further discussion of patterns of victimisation in Chapter 4). Such a degree of localisation also appears to exist in Akron, Ohio where 76 per cent of burglary suspects live in the same census tract as their victims, though rather fewer (11 per cent) in the same street block group (Pyle, 1976a). There is some evidence (Brantingham and Brantingham, 1975b) that burglars move to the fringe of their neighbourhood (or into the fringe of the next one) to commit their crimes. This accords well with the opportunist thesis mediated by the fear of recognition.

Much of this contradicts the popular image of the burglar. This would have him attacking the detached houses of the wealthy at dead of night while the occupants are asleep. He will know what he has come for, even where to find it, and will deal expertly with alarms and other security devices. These myths are not without foundation. They refer to the 'professional' thief – the older, more skilled, careful burglar who certainly exists but who is numerically swamped by his brash young opportunist colleagues. Baldwin and Bottoms (1976) highlight the contradiction for Sheffield (Table 1.12). We can see that the vast *majority*

Table 1.12: Housebreaking and Rateable Values: Sheffield, 1966

Rateable value	Estimated no. of housebreakings	Rate per 1000 dwellings
⩽£30	350	6.0
£31-56	440	6.6
£57-100	208	5.9
£101-200	144	23.4
>£200	28	51.9
Not known	44	–
Total	1214	7.0

Source: Baldwin and Bottoms (1976), Table 6.

of housebreakings (82 per cent) involve dwellings with a rateable value of £100 or less. Higher-valued dwellings are, on the other hand, subject to greater *risk* of housebreaking: these are the ones attacked by the small band of professionals. If we find that these are located in peripheral districts, this accords well with Reppetto's (1974) comments that affluence is a factor only in such locations. Baldwin and Bottoms found that this contradiction only applied to burglary. Thefts from prepayment meters are correlated with low rateable values and other residential thefts have no particular association with house values. In a sense the patterns of offending of the professional thief tend to contradict the notion of a homogeneous group, yet they are in such a minority (except perhaps in super-affluent metropolitan districts) that the degree of disturbance entailed is minimal. So much so that police response to burglary calls is only marginally affected by prior perceptions of the type of dwelling involved (Conklin and Bittner, 1973).

So we can see that even in this restricted case of residential theft there exists a complex interaction between the characteristics of the offender and the situation of the offence, which determines the resultant spatial pattern. Moreover, we would be wise to remember that the clear-up rate for residential theft is extremely low (four per cent in Boston; 30 per cent in Birmingham, though in Birmingham about one-third were cleared by arrest or summons so the comparable figure to Boston is about ten per cent). At the same time, a high proportion of residential theft – Sparks *et al.* (1977) report 68 per cent for property offences in their London areas – is simply not reported for reasons we will return to in Chapter 4.

(b) Non-residential Burglary

A considerable difficulty in assessing rates of non-residential burglary lies in determining the appropriate target population. The targets in this case are shops, offices, warehouses, factories and schools, etc., each of which is clearly differentially distributed throughout the city. To calculate the rates on the basis of population is erroneous and can lead to misleading geographical patterns. Yet this is what many authors have done, usually implicitly by treating burglary as a single category. The notable exceptions are Boggs (1965), Phillips (1973) and Baldwin and Bottoms (1976). Phillips gives a neat illustration of the differences in business burglary and robbery rates in Minneapolis based on population compared to those based on employment (Figure 1.8). Population-based, business burglary and robbery appear to be an inner-city phenomenon. Related to the distribution of jobs it appears quite the reverse,

Figure 1.8: Business Burglary and Robbery Rates: Minneapolis, 1971

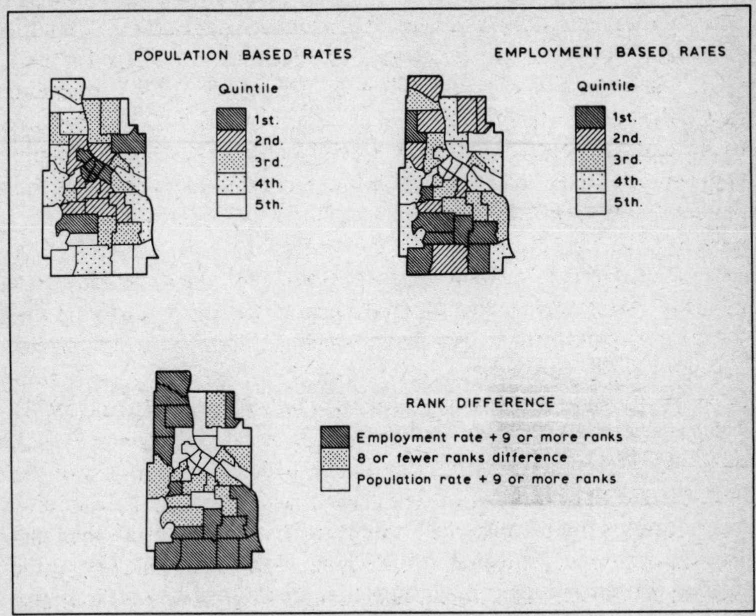

Source: Phillips (1973), Figure 1. Reproduced by permission from *Proceedings of the Association of American Geographers.*

with the highest rates on the periphery. However, even employment-based rates may be biased since newer premises in peripheral areas tend to be more labour and capital intensive than their inner-city counterparts.

In her study of St Louis using crime-specific rates, Boggs (1965) concludes that non-residential burglaries are part of a pattern of crime quite different from crimes of violence and those against residential property. She suggests that business targets most at risk are those in proximity to offender areas. As we shall observe in the next chapter, this means a concentration in the inner zones of cities – a situation confirmed by Lambert (1970) for Birmingham (Table 1.13, Figure 1.9). The pattern applies to all types of theft from non-residential premises but is strongest for burglaries of business premises other than shops.

So again we see here the opportunity paradox. The *risk* of burglary to business premises is higher in suburban areas, perhaps because in

Table 1.13: Distribution of Thefts from Non-residential Property: Birmingham, 1966-7

Type of theft	Inner-city No.	%	Middle zone No.	%	Periphery No.	%	Total No.	%
Cloakroom thefts from premises	68	56	27	27	27	22	122	100
Thefts from yards, building sites	28	52	9	17	17	31	54	100
Thefts from business premises[a]	103	71	24	16	19	13	146	100
Burglary of business premises (excluding shops)	63	79	8	10	9	11	80	100
Burglary of shops and other non-residential thefts[b]	100	67	20	13	30	20	150	100
Total	362	66	88	16	102	18	552	100

a. Not including shoplifting.
b. The zonal distributions of these two categories are not given separately. The figures given here are achieved by deduction from Table 36. The number of shop burglaries is given in Table 9 as 106.
Source: Lambert (1970), from Table 8.

such locations the premises may offer greater rewards to the thief and may be less well protected against him. *Numerically*, however, the greatest concentrations of such burglaries are in inner-city areas, partly because the targets are more numerous, but also because of proximity to the haunts of the casual thief.

(c) Shoplifting

The distribution of shoplifting offences can only be understood in relation to the special circumstances which surround its reporting. The rules of evidence in British courts demand that the offender be seen not only to remove the goods but also to leave the shop without paying. Convictions are normally obtained only when the offender is apprehended after leaving the shop. Fulfilling these conditions is more difficult if not impossible for the small shopkeeper. Another factor is the role of the police. Shops are private property and therefore cannot be patrolled by the police, who nevertheless must be responsible for any charge. So the shopkeeper or his agent must detain the offender until a policeman arrives to take particulars, at which point the charge may be accepted or rejected. The results of these procedures is a virtually 100 per cent clear-up and conviction rate for reported shopliftings, which predominantly come from chain and department stores large enough to employ store detectives. Thus the distribution of reported shopliftings is almost certainly dependent on the location of such stores – the city

Figure 1.9: Approximate Location of Non-residential Thefts: Birmingham, 1966-7

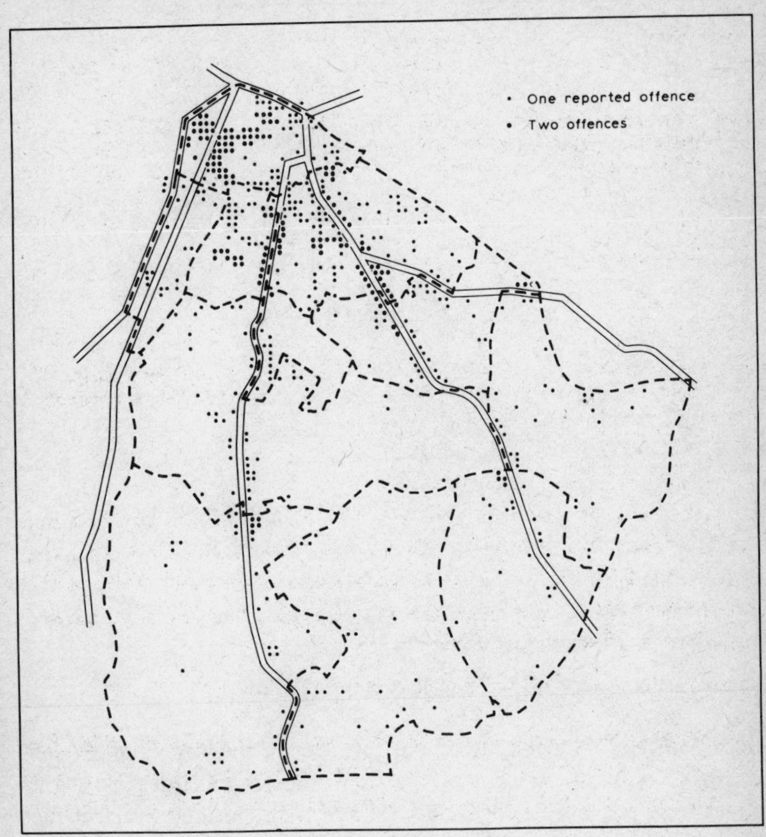

Source: Lambert (1970), Map 9. ©IRR, 1970.

centre, major suburban parades and large out-of-town shopping centres. Unfortunately, there are no studies which observe the general incidence of this common offence although analyses have been carried out for high-school students (Hardt and Petersen, 1968) and for supermarket offenders (Won and Yamamoto, 1968). My own data for Hull reveals a distribution (Figure 1.10) largely dominated by city-centre locations. City-centre shops were the scene of 67 per cent of the shoplifting offences reported in Hull in 1972 and these offences accounted for 79 per cent of the total value of goods stolen. According to the 1971 Census of Distribution, these shops accounted for 49 per cent of the

Figure 1.10: Distribution of Shoplifting Offences: Hull, 1972

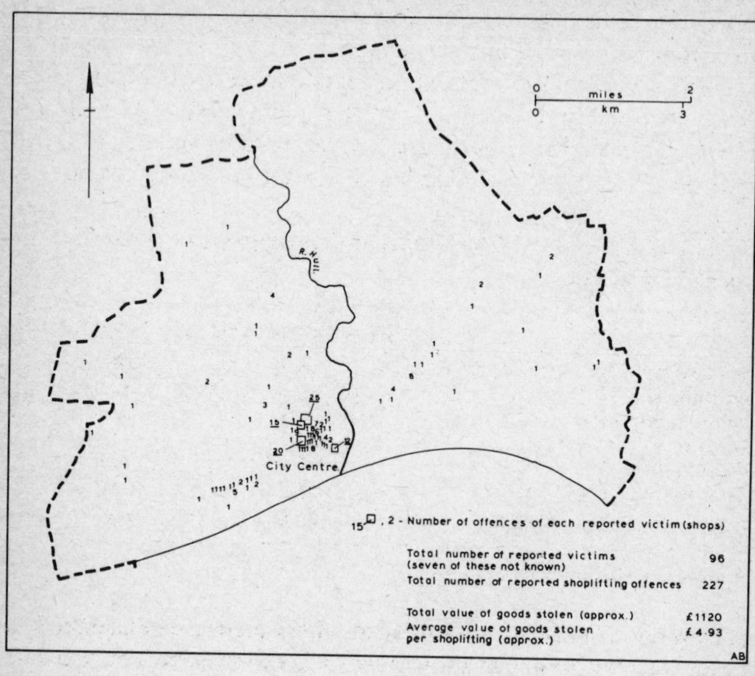

Source: Author's survey, 1 in 7 sample of reported offences.

floorspace and 41 per cent of the turnover in the city although consisting of only 14 per cent of the total number of outlets. Just four stores were responsible for 32 per cent of the reportings – a fact that illustrates the problems of relying on the official record for this particular offence. The true distribution of shoplifting is certainly not revealed by this map.

(d) Thefts Involving Vehicles

As many as one-third of property offences involve vehicles but within this group there are wide variations in spatial incidence. Those involving cars or motorcycles tend to reflect the distribution not so much of the vehicles but of storage and parking facilities. *Theft of a vehicle* is heavily concentrated in inner-city areas, not because there are more cars there (vehicle ownership rates are certainly lower) but because the cars are perforce left on the street. In addition, these areas frequently absorb the surplus demand for city-centre parking during working hours. Since the passing of legislation requiring new cars to be fitted with steering locks, the professional car thief is increasingly turning to the target of the older car (Mayhew *et al.*, 1980) which is more likely to be found in poorer, inner-city districts.

Thefts from a vehicle are similarly opportunity-specific. In an interesting study of an extreme form of this offence, Ley and Cybriwsky (1974) indicate that car-stripping has specific micro-locational correlates (see Table 1.14). The risks are clearly greater where the vehicle is

Table 1.14: Micro-locational Setting of Car-stripping in an Inner-city Area of Philadelphia

Setting	% of street frontage	% of stripped cars
Doorless flank of residence/commerce	18.5	20.3
Institution	16.7	22.5
Vacant residence	7.9	20.3
Commerce (whether vacant or in use)	14.3	6.5
Vacant/parking lot	1.6	13.0
Occupied residence	41.0	18.1
Total	100.0	100.0

Source: Ley and Cybriwsky (1974).

not overtly supervised nor associated with a particular residence. The authors do not comment on whether it is the abandonment which is connected with these locations or the subsequent theft and vandalism. Intuitively, the latter seem more likely. Theft of radios and other property from a car is similarly associated with anonymous locations.

Cycle theft is an awkward offence to discuss. A large proportion are commonly classified as 'no crime' by the police usually when the cycle is recovered undamaged within a few days. Lambert (1970) reports this as 25 per cent in Birmingham: in Hull, where ownership and use of cycles is greater, it is one-third (Coleman and Bottomley, 1976). Few studies have reported specifically on the location of this offence although Lambert comments that cycle thefts tend to occur more often in peripheral areas (regrettably he does not tell us from which areas the cycles are recovered). A situational classification of locations would prove most enlightening. Almost certainly, cycle thefts from in and around residential property will involve juveniles as victims and offenders. Adult cycles are more likely to be stolen from the vicinity of shops and workplaces. 'No crime' cycle thefts could well have different situational attributes as the motive may be conveyance rather than pure theft.

(e) Other Theft

This residual group is large (see Table 1.11) yet so varied as to beggar description. Some locational patterns will be clearly demarcated, others less so. For example, *theft from the person* (pickpocketing) tends to occur in places of public assembly – football grounds, racetracks, fairgrounds or busy shopping streets. *Theft by an employee* will be concentrated in industrial zones as will petty *pilfering* not involving breaking-in. Dockland and other areas where goods are stored in transit are also subject to this sort of casual theft, the extent of which is highly underestimated by official figures (Ditton, 1977). Other types of offence are so situationally variable as to present less marked spatial concentrations. *Thefts of handbags, purses, wallets and unattended clothing* take place in such varied locations as hospitals, pubs, theatres, factories and shops. Some of these categories may be sufficiently numerous to merit individual attention. What remains are all the oddball thefts none of which are very common but which together add up to a fair number. Thefts in Hull have included such diverse objects as beer tankards (perhaps only the reporting is rare!), a bunch of daffodils from public display, garden gnomes, four pairs of jeans (from a washing line) and the brake blocks from a policeman's bicycle.

(f) Handling Stolen Goods

This offence has received little attention in the literature, certainly as far as its spatial dimension is concerned. It appears to be used in two rather different circumstances by the police. The first, more obvious and probably numerically predominant, is to deal with professional receivers. However, it is also used, with police discretion, as a charge for offenders 'caught in possession' where there is inadequate evidence of the actual theft. This dichotomy is reflected in the location of handling offences in Hull. The majority occur in two very small areas of the inner-city. The remainder are fairly widely spread throughout other parts of the city where offenders live. It is no coincidence that this offence tends to be concentrated in areas where rates of theft are high and where the thieves also reside. The professional receiver is a key figure in the development and maintenance of 'criminal areas' to be discussed in Chapter 3.

(g) Fraud, Deception and Other Breaches of Trust

Any analysis of this rather varied group of offences is bedevilled by the factor of institutional immunity (Bottomley, 1973). This is the tendency of the victim (commonly an employer, bank, shop or other institution) to seek redress by other means than the law. Thus only a minute fraction of trust offences surface among reported crimes. Those that do tend to be more serious or involve an anonymous but apprehended offender. Distribution of these offences in Hull shows a high proportion in the city centre with cheque and credit card frauds most common.

(h) Criminal Damage

This offence has increased dramatically in Britain over the past decade or so. Until 1978, the rise was primarily due to inflation as more incidents qualified as indictable offences by exceeding minimum value of damage set by statute. The 1977 Criminal Law Act redefined all acts of criminal damage as serious offences, trebling overnight the number of offences, but removing a large part of the inflationary increase. Thus defined, criminal damage is now more than three times as common as personal violence in Britain (see Table 1.1). There are no studies of this offence: it is now more than ever rather artificially separated from the general run of vandalism.

(i) Arson

Arson has two distinct environmental situations. Traditionally it is one of the most typical rural offences. Nowadays it is, in America in particular, rapidly becoming a widespread urban offence. Traditionally arson was regarded as evidence of severe mental disturbance in the arsonist, nowadays the motives may include insurance fraud or political gesture. Hurley and Monahan (1969) suggest that the prime targets are commercial property, dwellings and barns/haystacks. Over 50 per cent of the arsonists in their sample knew the owner of the target. However, their sample was drawn from the inmates of a psychiatric prison and their comments may well be appropriate only for the traditional arson situation. Urban arson needs a rather different set of criteria for explanation.

2 OFFENDERS IN THEIR ENVIRONMENT

In this chapter we view the spatial distributions from the residential location of offenders. With a few exceptions the studies reported are again largely based on official records and subject to the attendant bias. In addition, the generally low clear-up rate for crimes introduces a further potential source of bias: the production of offenders may reflect clear-up procedures themselves as well as the overall incidence of crime. We will return to this issue in Chapter 4: in the meantime the reader should bear with these limitations.

Gross Offender Rates: Regional and Inter-urban Variations

Gross offender rates based on official aggregations suffer from an additional difficulty: offenders are usually processed in the police jurisdictions where the offence was committed and not where they live. The extent to which cities and regions import or export crime is little known. Media impressions certainly suggest that the growth of motorway and freeway networks has increased the mobility of criminals in both Britain and the United States. McClintock and Avison (1968) conclude of England and Wales that there is great variation in known offender rates between police force areas but that there is little evidence of a trend towards greater uniformity in the pattern. Since they also indicate that local clear-up rates vary considerably (from 21 per cent to 74 per cent in 1965), the difficulties and dangers of drawing general conclusions about gross offender rates at the highly aggregated regional or inter-urban level are clear. The situation in the United States is likely to be no better because of the greater fragmentation of police authorities and the greater consequent variations in police finance, manpower and professionalism. For these reasons, no attempt is made here to discuss the broad sweep of offender rates. Fortunately, in the more circumscribed studies discussed below, efforts have been made to ensure that rates are appropriately area-specific in residential terms.

Different Types of Offender

(a) Age and Sex

Comparative studies of the spatial distribution of offenders by both age and sex are rare. Baldwin and Bottoms' (1976) work on Sheffield approaches the ideal though they were unable to split females into age groups for lack of numbers in the sample. Figures 2.1 and 2.2 show the

Figure 2.1: Adult Male Offender Rates: Sheffield, 1966

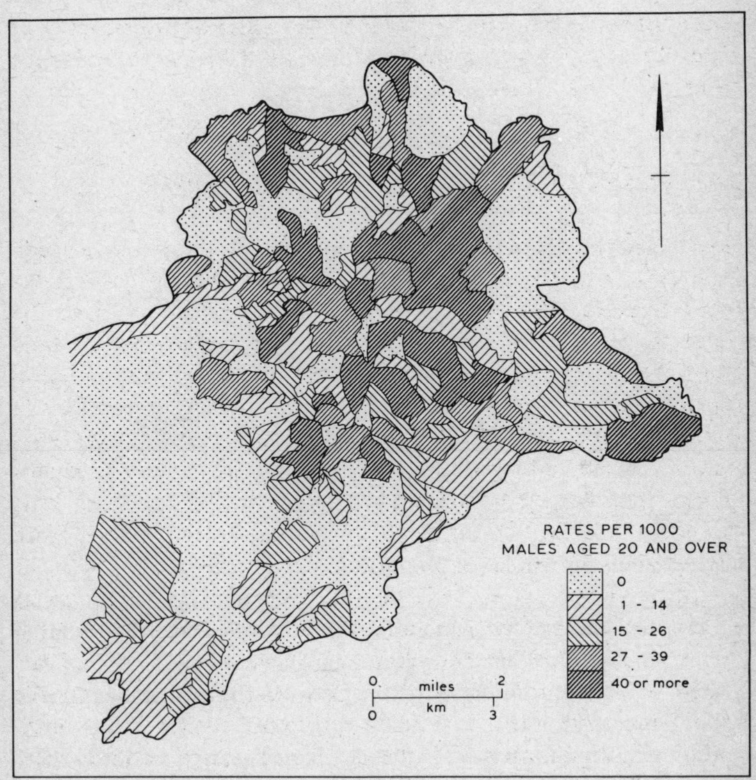

Source: Baldwin and Bottoms (1976), Map 3.

rates of adult and juvenile male offending in Sheffield. The concentric ring pattern of offences is not nearly as evident for offenders. Baldwin and Bottoms (1976, p. 77) conclude that 'offenders tend to be concentrated in:

Figure 2.2: Juvenile Male Offender Rates, Sheffield: 1966

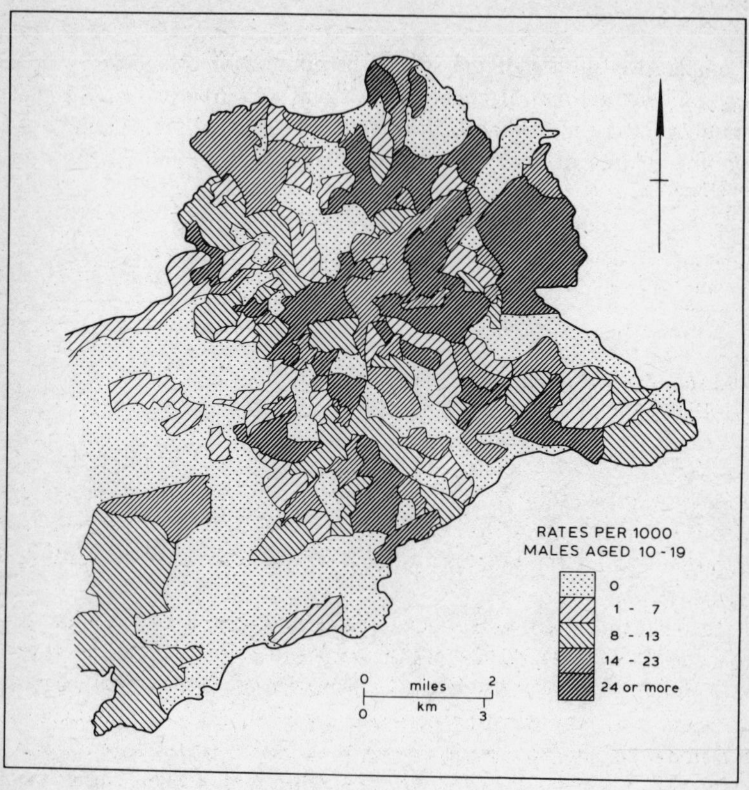

Source: Baldwin and Bottoms (1976), Map 4.

(a) the so-called 'twilight areas' with relatively high proportions of Irish and/or Commonwealth immigrants;
(b) some enumeration districts adjacent to the main areas of heavy industry; and
(c) on (certain parts of) particular council estates, especially those built in the interwar years.'

Baldwin and Bottoms' main thesis is that housing tenure is a key factor in the differential distribution of offenders in the city. They calculate offender rates for areas grouped by tenure (Table 2.1). While the rates are highest in the private rented areas (mostly nineteenth-century inner-city districts), the differential over some peripheral areas of

Table 2.1: Offender Rates by Age, Sex and Tenure Type: Sheffield, 1966

	Enumeration districts with more than 50 per cent				
Offender rates[a] (per 10,000 relevant popn)	Council housing	Private rented	Owner occupied	Mixed tenures	All districts
All offenders	30	33	12	22	23
Females	10	10	5	10	8
Males	50	56	20	36	40
Adult males (20+)	29 (31)	35 (38)	11 (11)	19 (18)	23
Juvenile males (10-19)	160 (144)	152 (153)	82 (66)	125 (124)	127

a. These figures are the mean of the rates for the enumeration districts in each tenure type. The true rates are only given for adult and juvenile males (figures in brackets). The rates refer to indictable offences only.
Source: Baldwin and Bottoms (1976), Tables 18 and 24.

council housing is by no means as marked as with the location of offences. The pattern is repeated by age and sex, though these rather broad groups do tend to conceal important variations, particularly among council estates where the rate for juvenile males is relatively high.

In a study of Newcastle-upon-Tyne dealing just with juveniles but concentrating on sex differences, Edwards (1973) shows that the incidence of delinquency is highly segregated spatially. The analysis is based on wards and for males the offender rate (for all offences, indictable and non-indictable) ranged from 180 to 1,450 per 10,000 relevant population, for females from 11 to 443. What is interesting about this study is that it indicates both similarities and differences in the sex distributions. Of the six most delinquent wards on the male rate, four appear also in the top six on the female rate. However, the second highest ward in the female list is only eighth in the male, and the fifth female ward is the 18th male. So while there is some confirmation here for Baldwin and Bottoms' conclusions that age and sex distributions are rather similar, there is a suggestion that male and female delinquents may *also* come from rather different environments. Regrettably, Edwards does not identify the location of the wards nor their character in anything except the broadest terms. Moreover, her sample size, especially for females, is much too small to make more than a very general comment on the spatial pattern.

Similar restrictions apply to the earlier work of Bagley (1965) on Exeter. Only four of the 16 wards on which he based the analysis had more than six delinquents in his sample. What is interesting about his findings is that 41 per cent of the delinquents in Exeter were resident in one ward, and all came from an inter-war council estate in that ward. In Exeter, as in Sheffield (see Baldwin and Bottoms, 1976, Table 31) and Leicester (Jones, 1958) there is considerable disparity between council estates even of the same age and house-type in terms of the offender rate, particularly for juveniles. Terence Morris (1957) identified reputation as a key differentiator of such areas, and in his work on Croydon labelled them as 'rough' and 'respectable'.

Lambert's (1970) study of Birmingham also covers the distinction between adult and juvenile males though he took 15 years as the critical age and was forced to use rather crude estimates of the relevant population. In so far as his rates are comparable, they confirm the general distributional patterns. Adult male offenders tend to be concentrated in inner-city areas, particularly those where multi-occupation of dwellings is common – the so-called 'zone in transition', or 'twilight area'. The rate is also above average in some peripheral council estates – especially, but not always, the older ones. It is in the latter type of area where male juvenile offenders have the greatest incidence, though they too are above average in inner-city areas. Both adult and juvenile males are least common in peripheral owner-occupied areas and in parts of the middle zone.

For female offenders, the spatial evidence is very scarce. One general conclusion from Edwards' Newcastle data is that the incidence of female offenders in the wards which show up as highly delinquent for males is not necessarily so extreme. In the case of shoplifting (by far the most common offence for females) the distributions shown for Hull in Figure 2.3 show considerable differences between the sexes in residential location (Davidson, 1976). Female shoplifters tend to come either from peripheral council estates, especially in East Hull, or from the middle-class, middle-zone areas of West Hull. In the former, the tendency is for the offender to be juvenile; in the latter adult. The council estates with the greatest concentration of female shoplifters are not generally those with a high incidence of male offending in other crimes. Curiously, young male shoplifters tend to reside, in Hull at least, in inner-city areas as well as in the peripheral council estates.

Wallis and Maliphant's (1967) analysis of the London boroughs is restricted to boys. They are able to show, even on this admittedly large-area basis, that juvenile delinquency is significantly correlated to a wide range of variables – housing, land-use, demographic structure, and social and economic conditions. Delinquency rates in 1961 were highest

Figure 2.3: Residential Distribution of Shoplifters by Sex: Hull, 1966

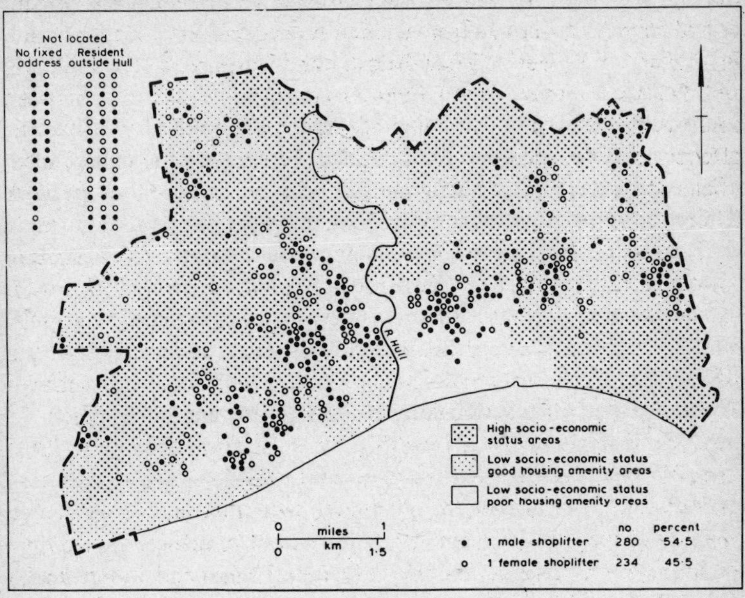

Source: Author's survey, all reported offenders.

in inner-city boroughs, particularly those fringing the business areas of the City of London to the north and east (Finsbury, Shoreditch, Stepney, Bethnal Green) and south of the River Thames (the northern sectors of Camberwell, Lambeth and Battersea). The most significant correlations were with social class (percentage of males in manual occupations) and overcrowding (persons per room). Slightly less important were lack of educational attainment, lack of household amenities and demographic change. In Blackburn, Lancashire, the most significant factors in the distribution of juvenile delinquents are poor housing amenities and overcrowding (McAllister and Mason, 1972). Juvenile delinquents, however, stand in contrast to children in care who are associated with a rather different cluster of variables including poverty, unemployment and married females in employment.

It seems fair to conclude that in most British cities one would expect to find a residential concentration of adult male offenders in the older, inner areas certainly in relative if not absolute terms. Juveniles of both sexes tend to be more prevalent on council estates, especially on older ones, but juveniles too may be concentrated in the inner-city. Adult females, much less numerous overall, are the least residentially segregated. The proviso must be made, however, that anomalies to this general pattern do exist and may be significant.

(b) Recidivism

One possible explanation for the differential distribution of offenders in cities is offered by the role of criminal networks in the transmission of criminal experience. This theme will be examined in more detail in Chapter 3, but it is useful to observe at this stage the pattern of recidivism since this may yield some clues to the distribution of criminal experience.

Baldwin and Bottoms' Sheffield study is again virtually the sole source of information on this topic. Their data (Table 2.2) serve to

Table 2.2: Rates of Male Offenders by Age, Recidivism and Type of Area: Sheffield, 1966

(Rates per 10,000 of relevant population) No. of previous convictions	Age 10-19				Age 20+			
	None	1-3	4+	Total	None	1-3	4+	Total
Type of area[a]								
Owner-occupied	42	19	5	66	4	3	4	11
Rented	92	46	15	153	12	15	11	38
Council	68	66	10	144	8	10	13	31

a. According to predominant tenure type.
Source: Baldwin and Bottoms (1976), Table 24.

refute the common assumption that recidivism is endemic only in the slums of the inner-city. While in these areas (shown by a predominance of rented accommodation in their typology) the overall offender rate is high, the rate for first offenders is also high for both adults and juveniles. For adults with four or more previous convictions, however, the highest rate obtains in council areas, where the highest rate for juvenile offenders with one to three convictions also occurs. It is clear, in Sheffield certainly, that council areas contain as high if not higher proportions of recidivists than the inner-city.

The results of my own survey of Hull lend some support to these conclusions although the distinctions between inner-city and council areas are much less dramatic. Table 2.3 presents a slightly different view on this issue. The base here is the number of cleared-up crimes rather than the number of offenders. This means that it is inappropriate to

Table 2.3: Percentage of Offences Committed by Recidivists and Multiple Offenders by Offenders' Residence Area: Hull, 1972

Percentage of cleared-up indictable crimes	By offenders: Known to have committed other offences within year (1)	With previous convictions (2)	With record of other offences (either (1) or (2))
Offender's area type[a]			
High status	70.9	34.3	74.2
Medium status	57.4	46.8	75.2
Low status: inner-city	67.1	55.9	82.6
Low status: council	66.3	45.5	80.5

a. According to socio-economic status and housing condition of residents.
Source: Author's survey.

calculate rates since each of the offences of offenders committing more than one offence will (if it enters the sample) be included separately. However, a clear estimate of the proportion of offences involving offenders with known criminal experience does emerge. A distinction is also made between recidivism (as measured by one or more previous convictions) and multiple offending which is taken as known to have committed other offences in the current year. The proportion of offences committed by recidivists is highest for offenders resident in inner-city areas where it reaches 56 per cent. Only 34 per cent of offences by residents of high status areas involve recidivists. The proportions of offences that are one of a series in the current year is much more evenly distributed – very similar in inner-city and council areas and, curiously, slightly higher for offenders resident in high status areas. If the two conditions are combined we find that the proportion of offences committed by offenders with other known criminal experiences is pretty tightly confined to the range from 74 per cent (high status areas) to 83 per cent (in inner-city areas).

These proportions are very high and give some indication of the extent to which crime is produced (in the official sense) by a small population of offenders who offend repeatedly. The theory that the inner-city slum becomes the residential environment for the long-term recidivist gains more support from my data than Baldwin and Bottoms', but their comment that it applies to a certain kind of adult recidivist and is far from the whole picture is entirely appropriate. At the same time, criminal experience as measured by the incidence of serial offending is by no means as differentially distributed as one might expect.

(c) Social Class

Socio-economic status and its rather vague relation social class have been the object of much speculation and rather less definitive study as a factor in patterns of crime. The imputation and common conclusion are that criminal activity is more prevalent among the lower social orders. Patterns of crime within a city will therefore merely reflect the spatial expression of class segregation. This is an important thesis and needs examination. The evidence comes from two rather different types of study: the 'ecological' analysis based on aggregated data for spatial units (wards, census tracts, neighbourhoods, etc.) and the non-spatial direct survey. Again we must rely on Baldwin and Bottoms (1976) to bridge the gap.

Taking the direct studies first, there is a general reporting of higher incidence of criminal offending among the lower classes. Douglas *et al.* (1966) took a cohort of births and followed their careers to the age of 17. By this age, 12 per cent of the boys had been involved with the law compared to 1.6 per cent of girls. For boys with fathers in professional and salaried occupations, the proportion was 4 to 5 per cent: for boys from semi- and unskilled manual backgrounds the ratio was just over 20 per cent. These figures are low by other standards (for example compared to the United States) cf. Ball *et al.*, 1964; Wolfgang *et al.*, 1972 or from self-report studies (e.g. Belson, 1975) but they represent class differentials fairly realistically. Reiss and Rhodes (1961) give delinquency rates for American white schoolboys as 3 per cent for those with high status fathers and 7.6 per cent for those with low. They also show that as a general rule the more delinquent the area, the higher is the delinquency rate among all status groups. There are considerable variations within the social classes which can lead to overlap in rates between them. For example, high status boys from a poor area may more likely be delinquent than low status boys from a good neighbourhood.

These findings are confirmed elsewhere. McDonald (1969) studies self-reported delinquency in four environmental contexts in London and the West Country. She found (Table 2.4) that while differentials between middle- and working-class children were maintained in all the areas, the proportion of children admitting to larceny varied between the areas. Thus 17 per cent of middle-class children resident in a working-class area of East London admitted thieving, only 11 per cent of working-class children from middle-class suburban London did so. These area differences were less evident for admissions of petty theft and school misconduct and not at all for criminal damage or violence,

Table 2.4: Larceny Admissions by Social Class and Area: London and the West Country, 1967

Area (predominant class composition)	Percentage children admitting serious theft middle-class	working-class
Surburban London (middle-class)	5	11
West Country (upper working-class)	5	9
North London (upper working-class)	12	17
East London (lower working-class)	17	20

Source: McDonald (1969), Table 5.4.

although class differences were maintained for all these offences.

Turning to aggregate analyses, there is a wealth of studies reporting in various ways the relationship between social class and crime rates (for example, Wallis and Maliphant (1967) on London; Brown *et al.* (1972) on a northern industrial city; Giggs (1970) on Barry, South Wales; Castle and Gittus (1957) on Liverpool: American cities covered include Philadelphia (Lander, 1954), Seattle (Schmid, 1960), Cleveland (Corsi and Harvey, 1975), Detroit (Bordua, 1958) to name but a few). These studies are comprehensively reviewed by Braithwaite (1979). Many more studies have used crime rates and social class among a larger set of social indicators. The findings are almost universal: crime rates correlate inversely with social class or socio-economic status, however measured.

These aggregate studies suffer from a number of disadvantages. First, there is the so-called 'ecological fallacy' which warns against assuming that relationships found at the aggregate level (ward or census tract) can apply at the individual level. Secondly, even if the correlation exists at both aggregate and individual level, it may still be spurious, i.e. the coincidental product of some other factor or process. For example, both criminality and social class may be produced by intelligence (or lack of it) or racial discrimination, and the simple fact of their association tells us nothing about the possible background causes. These are traps for the unwary which, if we have taken the point of figures quoted from McDonald above, we should no longer be. To rely on simple correlations, however sophisticated the analysis and interpretation, is not sufficient. It is this situation that Baldwin and Bottoms are at pains to avoid.

In their Sheffield study the patterns at both aggregate and individual level are observed. The relevant offender rates in the city as a whole are calculated to be 0.06 per cent for non-manual workers,

0.25 per cent for skilled manual workers and 0.63 per cent for semi- and unskilled manual workers. The fact that these rates are low compared to those already quoted arises because they derive from cross-sectional data (one year) rather than over a criminal career. In Table 2.5 their breakdown of the rates for semi- and unskilled workers by

Table 2.5: Area- and Class-specific Rates of Offending for Employed Males: Sheffield, 1966

% of area's population in semi- and unskilled manual work	Semi- and unskilled manual offenders rate per 1000 relevant population in			
	All areas	Council	Rented	Owner-occupied
15	31	NA	NA	31
15-25	48	36	50	47
25-35	56	61	102	29
35-45	68	74	58	67
45	85	96	70	NA

NA = no areas of this type.
Source: Baldwin and Bottoms (1976), Table 22.

types of area is given. The overall pattern is that the lower the socio-economic status of an area (i.e. the higher the proportion of semi- and unskilled workers) the higher the incidence of offending in this group. A similar pattern occurs in areas dominated by council housing. For rented areas, however, the highest rate obtains in the middle of the status range, i.e. those rented inner-city areas containing fair proportions of higher class groups. There may well be a ready explanation for this, since the most unstable of inner-city areas generally contain a transient element of skilled or professional people in the early stages of their careers, whereas those inner-city areas with the highest proportion of semi- and unskilled workers are more likely to be the stable, socially cohesive slum neighbourhood. This is an important distinction and one we will return to in the next chapter. The rate of offending among low status individuals in owner-occupied areas is less conspicuously different from the general pattern. Here it is the low rate in the middle of the range that draws comment but the differences are probably not sufficiently large to be significant. Baldwin and Bottoms also observe the pattern for skilled manual workers (there are not enough non-manual offenders to consider their distribution). Here the evidence is less equivocal: for all types of area, rates of offending decrease with social status. So Baldwin and Bottoms leave us with some confirmation of the earlier comments but highlight one or two anomalies from the general pattern.

This consideration of the distribution of offenders by social class leads to the conclusion that two quite distinct factors are operating: the class of the offender and the class of his residential environment. It seems that, irrespective of their own position in the social order, individuals are more likely to offend if they live in a low-status neighbourhood. At the same time, offending is likely to be more prevalent among the lower status groups in any one neighbourhood. The result is bilateral variation in offender rates with the highest rates occurring among low status people in low status areas and the lowest rates among high status individuals in better areas. Between the extremes the rate can be produced by either individual or neighbourhood factors – a situation that may do much to explain the dfficulties and confusion in studies relying upon simple correlations. John Braithwaite has provided an empirical test of these patterns for juvenile delinquency in Brisbane (Braithwaite, 1979). A breakdown (Table 2.6) of officially recorded

Table 2.6: Area- and Class-specific Delinquency Rates: Brisbane, 1969-73

Male juvenile delinquency rate per 1000 relevant population

Social class of area	Social class			
	High	Medium	Low	Total
High	9.9	16.8	39.0	19.2
Medium	12.6	18.4	47.9	26.1
Low	20.2	32.3	72.4	46.9
Total (N = 2300)	12.6	22.0	55.8	30.4

Source: Braithwaite (1979), Table 7.3.

delinquency by social class of area and social class of individuals demonstrates that both have a negative relationship with delinquency rates. Individual class effects are the stronger judging by the degree of disparity between categories. Both effects are independent but combine to exaggerate differences between areas. In the British context, it also seems clear that consideration of social class should involve not just socio-economic status but housing status at both individual and neighbourhood levels.

We can, I think, reject the notion that patterns of offending simply reflect the distribution of social classes in cities. However, the extent to which class differences are a direct or indirect cause of crime and the balance between individual and neighbourhood influences are matters for continuing debate.

(d) Race

We now turn to an even more contentious issue. Are there racial differences in offender rates, and to what extent do these provide an explanation for the spatial patterns of offending which we have observed in cities? The situations in Britain and America afford both parallels and contrasts.

In the United States the *Uniform Crime Reports* give arrest rates for various racial and immigrant groups. For Index (i.e. serious) crimes in 1968, the rate for whites was 537 per 100,000 relevant population: for blacks it was 2,972 and American Indians 2,146. Among the Chinese and Japanese immigrant communities it was 306 and 300 respectively. So in America, black arrest rates are over five times the white. In Britain, the racial composition is very different, with a much lower proportion of coloureds who have rather different origins. Unfortunately, race is not consistently recorded in British crime statistics: Stevens and Willis (1979) have, however, reviewed arrest rates for indictable offences in London. For blacks, the overall rate was 3,961 per 100,000 population in 1975 compared to 1,249 for whites and 1,253 for Asians. These rates are not comparable to those of the American *UCR* ones quoted above, being based on total population and on a different, slightly wider range of offences. What is comparable is the rather lower differential in London, just over three times, between blacks and whites.

Despite the fact that race is a key variable in studies of urban social segregation (Peach, 1975), there is a dearth of evidence on the residential distribution of offenders by race. Since we know that coloured people tend to be segregated in particular parts of cities – more evident in the American ghetto than in Britain – it is reasonable to assume that coloured criminals are no less segregated, but we don't know and this is a vital consideration. As an alternative, let us review the relevant conclusions of race and crime studies and attempt to infer the environmental implications. There are three relevant issues: possible differences in the types of crime committed by racial groups; variations in the situations where they are committed; and consideration of age, sex, social status, etc.

In both the United States and Britain there is evidence that racial minorities tend to be more involved in crimes against the person as opposed to property offences. This occurs despite the contrasting relations between the minorities and the white majority in overall crime rates. In the United States, the *Uniform Crime Reports* show that the general differential between black and white crime rates is exceeded for homicide, rape, assault and robbery. Larceny differentials are markedly lower, burglary and auto theft about average. In London, the proportion of black arrests for crimes of violence is about twice the average, for burglary and other theft about average and for auto crime and trust offences rather below average (Stevens and Willis, 1979). For Asians, the major deviations are a high rate for assaults and shoplifting and a low rate for burglary. In Bradford (McCulloch *et al.*, 1975), the only offence groups in which minority rates (in this case Asians) exceed the white majority are woundings and sex offences.

The involvement of racial minorities in crimes of violence is elaborated by two further British studies, those of McClintock (1963) in London and Lambert (1970) in Birmingham, both of which deal with situational aspects. They reveal significant differences in the type of violence involved. Table 2.7 summarises McClintock's findings.

Table 2.7: Violent Crime and Birthplace: London, 1960

Type of violence			Birthplace	
	UK	Eire	Commonwealth	Elsewhere
Sex offences	+	--	+	-
Attacks on police				
Domestic disputes	-	+	++	-
Fights in pubs	+	+	--	+
Attacks in streets	+	-	-	

(++) + = (much) higher)
(--) - = (much) lower) than average proportionate involvement.

Source: McClintock (1963), Table 70.

Commonwealth immigrants are most heavily involved in domestic disputes and sex offences. They are rather less involved in incidents in public places, particularly pubs where others have noted the care taken by West Indians to avoid bodily contact in crowded situations (Sparks *et al.*, 1977, p. 233, note 6). The Irish, too, are over-represented in domestic disputes but also in pub incidents. On the other hand, they are rarely involved in sex offences. Lambert's Birmingham data relates to a less serious level of interpersonal incidents (Table 2.8). He also disaggregates the domestic group and country of origin of Commonwealth immigrants. We can see, therefore, that distinctions exist between Asians and West Indians within the domestic category. West Indian disputes tend to revolve round family and neighbours whereas such incidents are very rare among Asians whose 'domestics' tend to

Table 2.8: Minor Disputes and Nationality: Birmingham, 1966-7

	Nationality							
Type of dispute	English	Irish	West Indian	Asian	Mixed Asian	Mixed West Indian	Other mixed + European	Not known
Landlord/ tenant	– –	–		+	++		+	–
Tenant/ neighbours	–	–	+				+	
Family	+	++	+	–	– –		–	–
Pub/cafe	–					–		+
Other (e.g. in shops, on buses, at work)		–	–					+

(++) + = (much) higher) than average proportionate involvement.
(– –) – = (much) lower)
Source: Lambert (1970), Table 18.

involve landlords. We can also see that the English are prone to family disputes, but much less so with neighbours and landlords. Mixed Asians have a more extreme patterns than pure Asians, a situation that has been found also in Bradford (Batta *et al.*, 1975) where delinquency among mixed Asian youths is five times that for both the pure Indian and Pakistani groups. In contrast mixed West Indians in Birmingham are least differentiated of all the groups, perhaps indicating that West Indians have rather fewer problems of assimilation, if only in terms of patterns of offending. Lambert and Batta *et al.* both demonstrate the very low involvement of the racial minorities in property offences, but in neither case are the numbers large enough to make a reliable estimate of situational differences.

For an example of the effect of background variables on differential rates of racial offending we can turn to an American locale. Green's (1970) study of Ypsilanti, Michigan is particularly interesting for its attempt to consider all the background variables together so that we can see how they interact. He also separates race and birthplace, a distinction which has not been consistently dealt with in British studies. In 1965 the overall arrest rate for negroes was nearly treble that of whites for more serious (Index) crimes and nearly double for other offences. In Table 2.9 Green's analysis of the rates for different categories of offender is summarised. In only three of the 12 categories is the negro rate higher than the equivalent white rate. Two of these are the rates for offences against the person by employed offenders, i.e. irrespective

Table 2.9: Racial Differences in Average Annual Arrest Rates among Types of Offender: Ypsilanti, Michigan, 1950-65

Offenders' background Birthplace	 Employment	 Type of offence	Difference in arrest rate between whites and negroes
Michigan	Employed	Against person	Negro rate higher
		Property	No significant difference
		Other	No significant difference
	Unemployed	Against person	Too few cases for analysis
		Property	No significant difference
		Other	No significant difference
Elsewhere (usually Southern states)	Employed	Against person	Negro rate higher
		Property	No significant difference
		Other	Negro rate higher
	Unemployed	Against person	No significant difference
		Property	No significant difference
		Other	No significant difference

Source: Green (1970), Table 5 (summarised).

of whether they were Michigan-born or migrated there. The other category is employed migrants committing other (usually minor) offences. None of the categories involving unemployed persons showed significant differences between whites and negroes. Green is able to conclude that racial disparities in arrest rate are primarily due to the distribution of occupational and birthplace characteristics rather than race. He imputes the residual differences in offences against the person to the 'southern violence' syndrome brought by migrants. Age and sex are not factors in the differences. This detailed analysis largely refutes the earlier conclusions of Moses (1947) who, in a study of Baltimore, had found that negro areas had higher crime rates than white neighbourhoods irrespective of their social and demographic structure. It demonstrates that most of the differences between negro and white crime rates can be explained in terms of socio-economic status and birthplace variations between the two groups.

What inferences may be drawn from these studies in regard to the distribution of offenders in the city? The most important relates to the frequently-made observation that there is much crime in areas where coloured minorities reside – in certain parts of the inner-city – an association emphasised in ecological analysis by high correlations (e.g. Quinney, 1964; Wallis and Maliphant, 1967). These correlations between race and crime are in fact either false (they don't exist) or spurious (they exist but are not directly linked). In Britain, they are largely false. Let me quote Lambert (1970, p. 125):

> The extremely low rate of involvement in crime and disorder among coloured immigrants, West Indian and Asian, when also adjusted for age and proportions in either sex, would appear actually much lower. This finding is the more striking bearing in mind . . . that there is more crime committed in areas where immigrants live than in other areas; and more offenders live in the areas of high immigrant population density than in other areas.

So in Britain the existence of racial minorities may actually diminish inner-city crime rates. In the case of American negroes, the link between race and crime is spurious. It is largely the numerical predominance of negroes among the least-paid, poorest-housed that produces the high rates. In addition, the neighbourhood effect discussed in the previous section is likely to be even more dramatic in a ghetto situation and boost rates even higher. Segregation is in itself a criminogenic factor.

A second inference is that race may be significant in the distribution of particular crimes. However, the specific cultural background of the offender must be considered. Thus the pattern of domestic violence in a city may be rather different if there is a large West Indian minority as opposed to Asian. The factor of culture is at best very complex and cannot be discussed in depth here. It is important to recognise, though, that racial minorities may differ not only in origin, but also in terms of speed and willingness to assimilate, internal social structure, age and rate of change in the community. A strong, cohesive community may be inclined to settle disputes internally without recourse to the police. For example, Chambliss (1975) shows the importance of an articulate middle-class element in the Japanese community in Seattle. Language may play an important role in preserving community identity and norms. Bamisaiye (1974) gives an interesting account of crime in Ibadan, Nigeria, where rather different cultural factors operate. In many cases, however, cultural differences do not just exist between racial groups: as we shall see in Chapter 4, variations in cultural indicators such as norms and aspirations form an essential part of explanations of spatial disparities in the incidence of crime.

Relations Between Offence Locus and Offender Residence: The Journey-to-Crime

We may have noted, during the course of this and the preceding chapter, a distinct similarity in the spatial concentration of offences and of offenders' residences. This is particularly clear at the urban scale where the incidence of both crime and criminals is higher in certain parts of the inner-city than elsewhere in the city. Is this association purely coincidental, or does it mean that criminals have a propensity to 'foul their own backyard'? The answer is probably neither: but let us look at the evidence.

In Philadelphia most juvenile offenders live a short distance from the locus of their offence (Turner, 1969). The median distance was only 0.4 miles: some 73 per cent travelled less than one mile, 87 per cent less than two miles. The distance travelled for offences against the person and street crimes (e.g. auto theft) tends to be greater. In Boston, it is younger, non-white offenders who are more likely to commit residential crimes in their own neighbourhood (Reppetto, 1974). These offenders are likely to be more opportunist, less skilled and less experienced than the older offender who travels further. In Cleveland, Ohio, property offenders tend to travel further than personal offenders – 3.70 km compared to 3.22 km (Pyle, 1976b). In a more dispersed city, Phoenix, Arizona, Stephenson (1974) calculates the standard distance separating offence and offenders, residence locations as 4.5 miles, much less than the 7.2 miles if offenders chose their targets at random within the city.

An additional insight into journey-to-crime is given in a study of burglaries in Tallahassee, Florida (Brantingham and Brantingham, 1975b) where the offence rate is found to be higher on the periphery or margins of neighbourhoods compared to their centres. The suggestion is that burglars will travel sufficiently far to minimise the risk of identification, but not so far that they have no perception or information about potential targets, etc. The distance travelled is indeed the expression of a complex interaction between the offender (his background, predispositions, knowledge, perceptions, etc.) and the target or victim (the risks, rewards, opportunities, attractions, etc.)

In their Sheffield study, Baldwin and Bottoms (1976) devote some attention to this topic, confirming the localisation of much criminal offending but also suggesting that there are sufficient disparities between locus and residence to merit their separate consideration. They show that age is indeed very important: it is the older offender who travels further. Similarly, the type of offence is highly differentiated with violence and sex offences most localised, fraud and taking and driving least localised. Within the larceny category, the greater the value of property stolen, the greater the distance. Offender's sex, social class, whether he had a criminal record and whether he committed his offence in a group or alone were all found to have little or no effect on the distance travelled. It was found, however, that the higher the offender rate of an area, the more localised is the crime; and that offences are least local in the strongest 'crime-attracting' areas (i.e. the city centre and adjoining commercial and industrial districts).

If one significant feature is to be abstracted from these patterns, it must be the variety which exists. There is no general pattern of journey-to-crime, save the tendency to move towards the centre of the city. In fact the patterns of movement are often extremely specific and need careful consideration of a wide spectrum of factors relating to the crime, the victim and the offender. By way of illustration, compare the trips made by shoplifters to those of burglars. In Figure 2.3 we have observed the residential distribution of shoplifters: we have also noted that most of their offences are committed in the city centre (Figure 1.10) – because that is where the shops are concentrated; where the shops are bigger and more crowded, but also more likely to employ store detectives; and where the shoplifter may go for quite legitimate activities. An analysis of the connections between locus and residence will almost certainly reveal an intensely radial pattern with a high correlation between distance travelled and distance of residence from the centre. Consider now Figure 2.4. Christchurch and Hull are similar in size and in incidence of crime, including burglary. Compared to shoplifting, burglary is much more localised: few burglars travel outside the main cluster of offending immediately to the east of the city centre. Very few burglars travel to the richer districts to the north and west of the city: likewise very few choose victims in the same street.

The purpose of this illustration is to indicate the dangers of over-generalisation. Nevertheless, the links between locus and residence are an essential component in criminal activity and can contribute vital insights into the concentration of offending in particular environments (Herbert, 1977a). These links, however, involve not just distance but also consideration of direction and of the environment of origin and destination. We may conclude that high rates of both offences and offenders in an area are rarely coincidental (unless the area happens to contain many non-residential opportunities). Nor, except in the case of juveniles, is offending *extremely* localised. The implication is, how-

Figure 2.4: Journeys-to-burgle: Christchurch, New Zealand, 1979

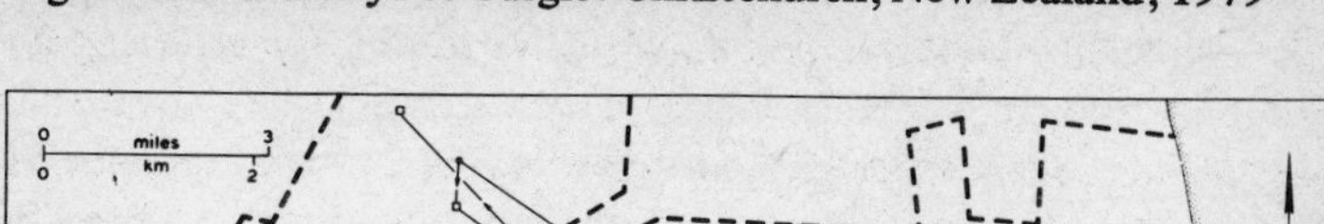

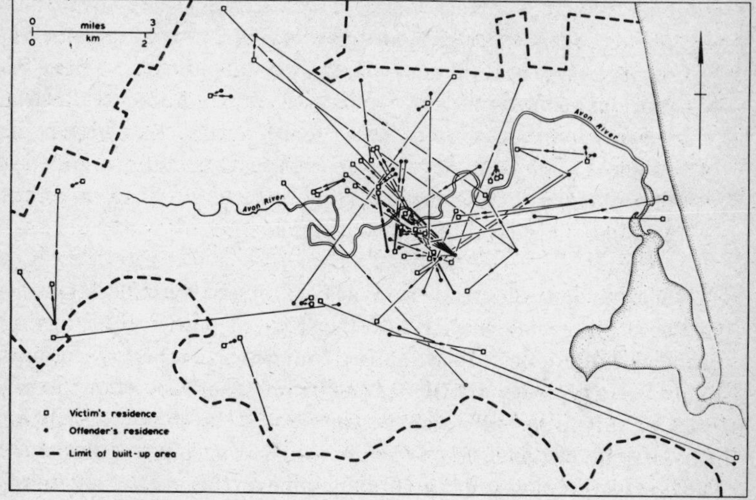

Source: Davidson (1980b), Map 2.

ever, that offences, while not committed on the offender's doorstep, nevertheless do tend to be located in the same sort of environment in which he lives.

Conclusions on the Distribution of Offences and Offenders

The purpose of this brief section is not to provide some generalisations about the patterns: this is the subject of Chapter 3. It is, rather, to set out some of the foundations for such generalisation. By now it must be clear that there exist considerable variations in the spatial concentration, both relative and absolute, of offences and offenders at all scales of analysis. Any generalisation must acknowledge this fact and its implications. In particular we should note:

(1) Gross offence and offender rates conceal more than they reveal, certainly as far as any attempt to explain spatial patterns is concerned, or perhaps more importantly in elucidating spatial effects in the incidence of crime. This comment applies whether it is the true rate or the official rate we are studying. The gross

rate can therefore only act as a very general guide to patterns of criminality and will tell us virtually nothing of relevance to understanding.

(2) As a corollary, ecological analyses involving gross rates must be suspect. We have already considered the danger of false or spurious conclusions in respect of racial differences. Such dangers exist on a wider scale among generalities about both offences and offenders. Crime is essentially such a diverse phenomenon that no theory can be expected to fit all cases nor explanation given without qualification.

If understanding of crime is to advance, there must be a retreat from the all-embracing analysis into the study of particular categories of crime and of criminal. I have chosen to treat these aspects according to a normative typology of offences and by reference to a set of characteristics of offenders fairly widely acknowledged as important. Other schema may be just as or more valid based on alternative typologies of criminal activity, for example according to the origins or motivations of the act, offender-victim relations or social reactions. Whatever criteria are adopted, contradictions will continue to emerge, some overt, some subtle, and should be acknowledged.

3 ECOLOGICAL AREAS AND CRIME

The identification of crime and of criminals with particular milieus is a long-established tradition in criminology. In the late nineteenth century Mayhew (1864) and Booth (1891) were describing the relations between crime, poverty and squalor in London. Equally long-established is the recognition among urban scholars of the varieties of environment within cities. The two traditions met in the Chicago 'School' of Human Ecology in the 1920s from which emanated developments in both theory and method that subsequently provided a continual source of stimulus. Since much of the ecological work on crime has been based on reported rates, it is appropriate to follow the discussion of offences and offenders with a review of the contribution of ecological studies to the understanding of crime-environment relations. At the same time the spectrum of ecological dimensions will provide a platform on which to elaborate a typology of ecological areas.

The Ecological Tradition

Rather than a blow-by-blow account of the development of the tradition, a useful summary may be achieved by examining the contribution of the two most important sets of contributors – the Chicago school and the modern factor analysts. For a more thoroughgoing review of the former, the reader should consult the excellent essay of Morris (1957): for the latter Baldwin (1975a) reviews British studies, and Wilkes (1967) concentrates on American studies. Baldwin's (1979) treatment is comprehensive.

(a) Chicago School

Although Shaw and McKay made the major criminological contribution within this school, they were in fact part of a much wider nexus of effort within urban social studies. The more general contribution of the Chicago school had two primary elements. First, it provided a series of generalisations about urban social structure. It was recognised that clear and obvious differences within cities existed over a wide range of variables describing the land-use, physical condition and demographic structure of neighbourhoods. The most significant observation was the zonal arrangements of many of these variables: high population densities and physical deterioration in the centre, low density and better conditions on the periphery. The general density gradient decreasing from the centre was found to apply to a larger number of American cities.

The second contribution was in method. The process of grouping individuals into a network of areas, on a grid or other system, and calculating rates for each area was the basis of the analysis. The association of the various phenomena was then described by visual and statistical correlation of the aggregate patterns. Meaningful generalisations about complex individual distributions could thus be achieved. A great deal of criticism has subsequently been levelled at this procedure, pointing out in particular the dangers of inferring individual relationships from aggregate data (we will return to this point later). Nevertheless, the original students of the Chicago school were more cautious about the interpretation of their findings than some of their later adherents. The positive gain was a significant advance in understanding of the urban system that may not have been possible without the generalising power of aggregation.

Shaw and McKay's (1942) achievement was to apply this method to delinquency data derived from court records and other sources and show that delinquency rates decline steeply from the city centre. In their own work on Chicago, this pattern was found to be consistent over a number of time periods. Later parallel studies showed its applicability in other urban areas. Differences in rates between areas were correlated with the physical condition of housing, income levels, demographic stability and ethnic status. Thus high rates of delinquency were likely in inner-city areas characterised by deteriorated, rented property, by high density of population, by large proportions of migrants into the city and by population loss to the suburbs. With some variation the pattern held then for adult and juvenile offenders, for males and females and even within particular nationality or ethnic groups. Recidivism was more prevalent among delinquents resident in high rate areas. Shaw and McKay inferred from their generalisations that the root of crime lay in some rather vague notion of social disorganisation. It was the breakdown of normal community relations in the deteriorating slums that led to high rates of delinquency. Lack of social institutions, overcrowding, poor standards of housing, weak social controls (arising from rapid turnover of population) led to or failed to prevent the development of criminal activity which once established becomes an enduring feature of such areas. Criminal skills and experience are passed on from one generation of delinquents to the next through a network of gangs and other forms of criminal association. Sutherland's (1939) more formal exposition of the theory of the cultural transmission of crime owes much to the diagnostic work of Shaw and McKay. Many later theories have been tested against their seminal empirical analysis.

(b) Modern Factor Analysis

The impact of this group is less clear-cut. Their work has been criticised, so severely at times that Hood and Sparks (1970) omit discussion of the ecology of crime on the grounds that it 'seems at the moment to be rather at a dead end'. Nevertheless, there is a considerable literature on the distribution of crime using factor analytic methods which cannot be ignored.

The early stimulus for these efforts came from Lander's (1954) publication of his analysis of crime rates in Baltimore. Again we find the contribution evolving on two points – in method and in theory. The methodological advance was in the application of multi-variate statistical techniques which allows the simultaneous consideration of a number of indices of crime and social conditions. Initially he selected seven: education, rent, home-ownership, sub-standard housing, overcrowding, non-whites and foreign-born. All were highly correlated to delinquency, but some were more important than others. Using multiple regressions and partial correlation, he suggested that the proportions of home-ownership and non-whites were of primary significance. A final stage was to use factor analysis to show that anomie, or social instability, rather than socio-economic status was the major determinant of the incidence of delinquency.

This theoretical conclusion about the relations between delinquency and anomie has been challenged perhaps most seriously (Baldwin and Bottoms, 1976) on the grounds that it is tautological, i.e. that the definition of anomie relies on concepts such as delinquency itself. However, Lander's work did stimulate a considerable body of comparative work. Some confirmed his findings (Polk, 1957; Bordua, 1958), others reaffirmed the primacy of socio-economic status (Chilton, 1964; Gordon, 1967), while yet others found varying relationships with economic status, family status and ethnicity using the Shevky-Bell model of urban social areas (Quinney, 1964; Polk, 1967; Willie, 1967).

Meanwhile Schmid (1960) in a study of Seattle considered an even larger number of social indicators deriving 18 from Census information and 20 from crime data. Eight factors were extracted and interpreted as the major dimensions of social differentiation in the city. The first four were identified as family status, occupational status, economic status and population mobility. Crime was variously associated with each but in Seattle was most clearly associated with economic status. Schmid found neither the anomie explanation nor the differential association concept derived from Shaw and McKay was appropriate. Later ecological analyses (e.g. Pyle, 1974; Smith, 1974; Corsi and Harvey, 1975; Mladenka and Hill, 1976) have continued to develop statistical sophistication without providing much theoretical clarification. Baldwin (1975a) is highly critical of similar British studies.

Ecological Dimensions: Opportunity Theories

Ecological studies have provided varying support for a number of postulates about the causes of crime. In this section the intention is to provide a synopsis of these in so far as they are relevant to the wider environment. We may define three rather diverse groups of hypotheses: a rather large set relating in one way or another to the concept of opportunity, and two rather smaller sets connected with anomie/social disorganisation, and sub-culture theory/differential association. The groups are by no means exclusive – there is inevitably at times considerable overlap between theories dealing with the same situation. Inevitably also, the treatment of some theories is curtailed by our concentration on environmental issues.

The idea that some environments provide more opportunity for crime is not new and we have seen ample evidence in Chapters 1 and 2 of the tremendous variations that exist. To treat opportunity as some monolithic concept is, however, fraught with danger. Terence Morris (1957) suggests a primary division which will serve us well: it depends on whether our focus of interest is on the offender or on the event itself.

(a) Predisposing Opportunities

These consist of factors which bear on the background environment of the offender. The theory is that some areas are more 'delinquency prone' than others (Herbert, 1977b). Such a concept underpins the generalisations of the Chicago school though their ideas were perhaps more tightly defined. Basically, the notion is concerned to point out that in certain areas there are influences at work which may increase the likelihood of an individual indulging in criminal acivity. Some of these influences will be the product of the home environment, such as poor supervision of children or inadequate socialisation within the family.

Others concern the social and physical fabric of the neighbourhood. It is with the latter that we are primarily concerned. Three themes are common among ecological studies:

(i) Social Status. It has been frequently noted that crime rates are high among the working classes. Social class bias in spatial patterns has been noted by Morris (1957), Reiss and Rhodes (1961), Clark and Wenninger (1962), Wallis and Maliphant (1967) and Basilevsky (1975) among others. While there is little doubt that areas predominantly occupied by the working class do have substantially higher rates of offending, it is clear from the material reviewed in the last chapter that the connection between crime and social class is at best indirect and at worst quite false. Nevertheless, as a diagnostic variable it does have some power so long as we are clear that in indicating areas where the incidence of offending is likely to be high we do not infer any causal connection. Braithwaite (1979) is equally cautious about making assumptions about the role of inequalities in wealth and power which underpin class differences.

(ii) Housing Conditions. Factors related to housing conditions are also regarded as important among predisposing factors. From Shaw and McKay through to the present, a poor or deteriorating residential environment has been seen to be concomitant with high rates of offending. In the last decade, the role of housing has been given more formal treatment through the emphasis of Rex and Moore (1967) on the recognition of specific housing classes in which there are intimate connections between tenure, housing amenities and the social, economic and legal constraints on access. One of the major conclusions of Baldwin and Bottoms' (1976) anaysis of Sheffield is the importance of housing tenure in explaining patterns of offending. That is, offending is much more common in high renting areas.

Another housing criterion regarded as predisposing is overcrowding. Here the debate has at times been quite fierce but inconclusive (see Freedman, 1972; Gillis, 1974; Roncek, 1975; Booth *et al.*, 1976; Higgins *et al.*, 1976). The root of the difficulty lies in the definition of crowding. Is it houses per acre, rooms per house or persons per room? The correlations and effects of each may be quite different (Winsborough, 1962) but no study has provided definitive links with crime. Yet this is an important issue and it is worth outlining some of the arguments. Two quite distinct approaches are evident (Fischer *et al.*, 1975; Freedman, 1975; Mercer, 1975): that of ethologists making inferences from animal populations and the more empirical explorations of crime and other social pathologies using aggregate data.

The ethological approach is typified by Calhoun (1962a, b, 1966), and has been popularised by such writers as Morris (1969) and Ardrey (1966). Essentially the argument is that as population density increases, there is a change in behaviour patterns which result in reduction in population growth. Thus rat populations develop a 'behavioural sink' – a group of rats whose behaviour is abnormal in some way: hyperactive, hypersexual, homosexual, cannibalistic or excessively passive. These rats will be crowded into a small part of the environment available and the remainder will be occupied by normal, breeding rats. Calhoun discusses in some detail the circumstances under which this phenomenon develops (they do vary so one may infer that the environment may have a mediating influence on the effect of density). Large cities are seen to be analogous to the crowded rat situation. The human 'behavioural sink' comprises political and social extremists (urban guerrillas, squatters, protest groups, etc.) together with deviant individuals such as the mentally ill, suicidal or criminal. The putative connection is that crowding leads to stress which in turn leads to one or more forms of deviant behaviour. Criticism has been levelled at the ethological argument on a number of counts. First, the validity of inferring human reactions from animal behaviour is questioned: human beings appear to have considerably greater powers of adaptation. Secondly, the implication that the behavioural response is unproductive or undesirable is refuted: crowding can have beneficial effects in stimulating non-deviant activity. As a corollary, the theory does not help to explain why there may be deviants in uncrowded situations nor how normal behaviour can emerge in crowded conditions at one place and time while the same conditions may elsewhere produce deviancy. What is lacking is an adequate definition of the social meaning of deviancy.

Empirical studies into crowding have been pretty consistent in reporting a positive relationship between delinquency and overcrowding. Some findings such as those from many ecological studies (Lander, 1954; Bordua, 1958; Chilton, 1964; Gordon, 1967) have been tangential to the main thrust of their argument. Others devote more specific attention to the crowding issues (Schmitt, 1957; Galle *et al.*, 1972; Freedman, 1972; Gillis, 1974). As Roncek (1975) points out in his review of density and crime, the empirical work has suffered from shortcomings of method which preclude an adequate unravelling of the links. In some cases, the effects of aggregation are not properly accounted for so the possibility of the ecological fallacy exists. In others, the variable(s) chosen to represent crowding are weak (e.g. taking gross density per acre). There is also a preponderance of studies dealing with juvenile delinquency and few relating to particular offences. Those studies which attempted to control for variation in other criteria, for example poverty or social status, have found the effects of crowding much weaker than those which did not. Roncek concludes that persons per room is more important a predictor of crime rates than population density but that even so the effects are smaller than other socio-structural variables.

Crowding is therefore an awkward dimension. Like social class it appears to have a straightforward association with crime rates in ecological terms, but at the individual level the connection is neither direct nor explicit. Cross-cultural studies have indicated wide variations in perceptions of personal space (Schmitt, 1963; Sommer, 1969); if replicated on a more localised level these variations could do much to account for the difficulties.

(iii) Social Environment. We are dealing here with a set of contexts which form the basis for social interaction outside the home. They include school, work, recreation and neighbourhood. The contexts of rather more periodic events such as holidays, excursions, etc. also provide predisposing opportunities too specific to be dealt with here. The significance of the social environment lies in the way in which an individual's behaviour is influenced by the values, attitudes and perceptions of the groups with whom he or she most commonly interacts. Schools are important because the peak incidence of (reported) offending is around the school leaving age. In their long-term study of delinquents in Tower Hamlets, London, Power *et al.* (1972) found wide variations (6-77 per 1,000 boys) in delinquency rates between schools in the area. They were, however, unable to find any correlation between the rates and attributes of catchment areas, educational attainment within the school or the type of school. Baldwin (1972) is sceptical of these conclusions on the grounds that there are inadequacies in the research method. However, Power *et al.* did find that delinquency rates were persistent within the schools over the 11-year study period. So whether or not the explantion lies within it, the school provides an environment which in some cases reinforces patterns of delinquency or in others inhibits them. McDonald (1969) also concludes that school, with social class and neighbourhood, influences delinquency. The reasons why this should be so are complex and no study has yet evaluated them. Hargreaves (1967) adopts a sub-cultural explanation, suggesting that in

schools there are likely to develop contrasting group situations. An academic sub-culture reflects teacher expectations and accepts the goal of achievement through examinations; a delinquent sub-culture is opposed to the dominant norms and allocates prestige through rejection of these norms. The division develops over a period of years and may be reinforced by timetables and streaming.

Work is an environmental context for crime that has hardly been studied. We know that large amounts of theft by employees go unreported (Home Office, 1973), that petty pilfering is rampant in many industries (Ditton, 1977) and that very little white-collar crime reaches the courts, so we know that the workplace is by no means crime-free. We may suppose that its environment therefore provides an important source of predisposing opportunity for crime not directly connected with work. The acquiescence of an employer to pilfering within his firm must reduce the inhibitions of his employees to other forms of petty theft outside the workplace. Not that this is necessarily a one-way process. An employer drawing his labour-force from an area where theft is common, even habitual, may find it hard to operate his business without a level of pilfering that elsewhere would be unacceptable.

There is also a considerable volume of evidence implying a connection between crime and leisure habits. One of the two peak times for offending is late evening (McClintock and Avison, 1968; Hindelang, 1976): the role of alcohol in crime is firmly established. We have already seen how many crimes of violence take place in or near cafes, pubs and other informal meeting places. For juveniles, the street or adjoining waste land may be the primary locale for recreation. In each case the distribution of such facilities or the lack of them may give us important clues to the pattern of crime. The concentration of offences in city centres may reflect not just the location of potential targets but also the fact that people are there for legitimate purposes. Many British peripheral council estates were built with inadequate social and recreational facilities. For crime this may have two consequences. First, it may lead to an amplification of delinquency among groups, particularly the youth, trapped by isolation in such estates. Armstrong and Wilson (1973) give a graphic account of such a situation in Easterhouse, Glasgow. Secondly, offenders may travel to the inner-city areas to commit their offences, not as a purposive act, but because the inner-city remains the focus of their recreational world.

Finally, there is the role of neighbourhood as a context for predisposing opportunity. In some senses it is invidious to treat neighbourhood independently from the other contexts of school, work and recreation since it may encompass all three. Yet there remain certain aspects of neighbourhood which are relevant to the explanation of differences in crime rates. These revolve round the development of neighbourhood norms related to criminality: the degree of tolerance towards crime or towards offenders; expectations of behaviour when confronted with an offence; attitudes towards police or other agents of justice; or simply perceptions of the prevailing moral code. The fact that the neighbourhood acts as a receptacle for such norms is a product of spatial constraints on behaviour and the social segregation endemic in urban life. That differences in patterns of social interaction between neighbourhoods exist is well-established (Irving, 1978). The content, duration, frequency and intensity of interaction vary considerably according to social status, demographic structure and length of residence as does the pattern of linkages.

In a study of Cardiff, Herbert (1976) considers differences between delinquent and non-delinquent areas on four counts. First, he finds that his description of the areas as locales for delinquent behaviour based on official statistics is confirmed by the inhabitants' perceptions. Secondly, while aspirations towards education are not consistent (some delinquent areas had high aspirations), educational attainment is markedly better in non-delinquent areas. More important perhaps from our perspective, he is able to show that definitions of delinquent behaviour vary, particularly with less serious offences which are much more likely to be tolerated (i.e. not reported) in the delinquent areas. Among serious offences, there are interesting disparities in attitude which could not be followed up. Finally, Herbert considers variations in parental sanctions and controls. Physical punishment is more common in the delinquent areas, verbal sanctions in non-delinquent areas – a pattern that generally holds over a range of delinquent acts. However, there are significant differences within the two groups of areas; for example one delinquent area showed a strong tendency to ignore the acts whereas the other delinquent areas were no different from the non-delinquent areas in this respect (see also Evans, 1980).

(b) Precipitating Opportunities

Precipitating factors relate to the circumstances surrounding the criminal act. The environment provides a variety of opportunities which may be influential in determining whether or not a particular crime is committed. The opportunities may be concerned with the target of the crime, with the activity of the potential offender, or with elements of the physical environment. Again we find that such opportunities are not randomly distributed in space.

(i) Targets. The range of potential targets available in an area is clearly important in determining the type and frequency of crimes committed there. We have seen in Chapter 1 that this applies more strongly to certain types of crime that are target-opportunity orientated, for example burglary and robbery. It is less true of other forms of violence and some types of theft where the situational aspects of the opportunity are of less relevance. Among ecological studies, these distinctions are rarely recognised and more often than not completely ignored. The exception is the work of Boggs (1965) on St Louis. She uses the standard procedures of factor analysis on area-based rates but defines the rates so that they are crime-specific. Thus the rate for non-residential burglary is based on the proportion of land-use devoted to business use, the auto-theft rate on the amount of space devoted to parking, etc. The results show a clear dichotomy between violence (excluding rape) and residential theft on one hand (where there are high correlations with offender rates) and non-residential theft on the other where there are few connections with the areas where offenders live. Rape and one of two miscellaneous theft categories fall outside the dichotomy and have few clear affiliations with the general pattern. The importance of Boggs' work is that it avoids the anomalies created by grossing up crime rates on the basis of population; for example the extremely high crime rates found in city centres are exaggerated by the few people who live there. Phillips (1973; see Figure 1.8) confirms how dramatic the divergencies may be when crime rates are not specifically related to targets.

On the whole, targets offer opportunities for crime in such a wide range of circumstances that it is almost impossible to generalise beyond the residential/non-residential dichotomy. However, it is important to recognise that it is not simply the location of a target that precipitates an offence, though this will happen from time to time with completely spur-of-the-moment offences. Normally targets only present opportunities when filtered by the offender's knowledge and perceptions, and we must know quite a bit about these before we can understand why some targets have a higher risk of being attacked than others. Nor is this a one-way process: the visibility or other attractions of a target may bring it within the range of perceived opportunities. The links can be further reinforced by the previous experience of the potential offender in that particular sector of crime.

(ii) Activities. Closely linked and complementary to the opportunities

offered by the location of targets are those related to the activities of the potential offender. Here we are not talking about activities directly connected with the criminal event itself, but those background activities which may precipitate an event by providing a platform or context for the involvement. Environments can provide such opportunities in a number of ways, some quite subtle, some more overt.

Perhaps the most obvious of the activity contexts is the gang or group. This may be formed quite deliberately for criminal purposes, but more often the group has a wider social function not necessarily nor explicitly connected with crime. This is a complex topic and one that cannot be adequately dealt with here. There is a considerable literature on delinquent gangs from Thrasher's (1927) original work on Chicago in the 1920s (for example see Cohen, 1955; Miller, 1958; Yablonsky, 1962; Ley, 1975). What is important to realise is that groups may generate norms and goals which may in some cases be realised through criminal acts. Take for example the adolescent peer group. Access to the group or acceptance as a fully paid-up member may involve some form of initiation rite: a test through which the novice must pass. The environment in which the group operates provides opportunities for tests and some may involve criminal acts: shoplifting from Woolworth's is a common form of peer status acquisition in Britain among young adolescents; forms of violence are more common among older youth. But even if the group does not require a criminal act as initiation, its activities on the streets and in the neighbourhood may lead to crime in a less formal way simply through the opportunities presented by the group and its patterns of interaction. To understand how these opportunities arise we need to know something about the dynamics of social interaction in a particular neighbourhood. At the same time, we may profitably concentrate on juvenile activities since it is here that the patterns are most critical, especially in connection with the first offence.

Individual behaviour also provides a springboard for criminal activity. We have seen how localised much crime is: part of the reason for this is the constraints imposed on the offender's knowledge of opportunities by the limits of his legitimate activities – work, shopping, socialising, recreation, etc. The greater mobility afforded by an affluent society brings a wider range of criminal opportunities within the consciousness of the potential offender. As we have already pointed out, increases in mobility imposed by government policy aimed at a fairer distribution of wealth or resources, for example slum clearance or New Towns, can have a similar effect. This is not to say that the most mobile members of society are likely to be the most criminal. This is certainly not true. But more mobile individuals, other things being equal, will be presented, because of their mobility, with greater opportunities for deviant activity.

(iii) Physical Environment. The influence on behaviour of the physical environment, buildings, spaces, layouts, etc., is now widely accepted in architectural and planning circles. The specific connections with crime rates were recognised by Jane Jacobs (1961) in her treatise on the American city. Despite the polemical nature of this book and its reliance on much anecdotal information, there emerges an unequivocal view of the links between crime and the physical environment. It centres round the notion that the public rather than the police are the crucial element in crime control and that ordinary citizens through their visible presence act to prevent crime in public places. Places and spaces not subject to the informal supervision provided by people going about their legitimate business are more likely to be the scene of crime. The distinction between public and private spaces is emphasised since it crystallises reactions to observed behaviour. Places which are neither clearly public nor private are particularly crime-prone.

Oscar Newman (1972) provides a more formal framework for Jacobs' ideas in his theory of 'defensible space', which he outlined in relation to observations of the location of crimes in housing projects in New York. Defensible space, he suggests (p. 50) revolves round four basic properties of the environment: (1) territoriality, (2) natural surveillance, (3) image and (4) milieu. Territoriality refers to 'the capacity of the physical environment to create perceived zones of territorial influence'. If the environment encourages inhabitants to assume rights of control over spaces it will be more secure. Natural surveillance is 'the capacity of physical design to provide surveillance opportunities for residents and their agents'. If non-private spaces, both indoor and out, can be casually and continually surveyed, security will be improved because intruders and/or victims are more readily identified. Image reflects 'the capacity of physical design to influence the perception of a project's uniqueness, isolation and stigma'. Distinctiveness in architectural detail both exterior and interior will promote residents' attachment to their environment as will architecture that is successful in symbolising life styles. A poor image will reinforce the alienation of the residents and increase their vulnerability to intruders. Milieu is concerned with 'the influence of geographical juxtaposition with "safe zones" on the security of adjacent areas'. Vulnerable spaces may be made less so by the physical proximity of secure activities, for example by being overlooked by residents observing from the safety of their homes.

The crux of Newman's thesis, that the environment provides differential opportunities for informal surveillance, is an attractive one which readily accords with our perceptions of the vulnerability of particular places to certain types of crime. We have already discussed in Chapter 1 how important this factor is in car theft and car-stripping. An American study (Pablant and Baxter, 1975) suggests that school vandalism is less where schools are more aesthetically attractive, more highly utilised by a diversity of activities, more readily overlooked by surrounding residents and in better illuminated neighbourhoods. In Britain a Home Office Research Project (Sturman, 1980) has investigated damage on buses and shown that its extent and location are clearly related (inversely) to the degree of supervision permitted by the internal layout. Mawby's (1977a) study of kiosk vandalism in Sheffield has similarly emphasised the visibility aspect. Indeed any short walk round the less genteel districts of a city will reveal a micro-locational distribution of graffiti well in accord with the defensible space hypothesis: on public property (road signs and other street furniture, public lavatories), on unsurveyed private property (gable ends, lock-up shops and garages, high-rise stairwells and lift-shafts), in inaccessible or unfrequented places (underpasses, car-parks) and so on. Yet even here some of the flaws in Newman's theory begin to appear. Graffiti are very common in bus and railway stations which could hardly be regarded as unfrequented or unsupervised, and a lot of vandalism and general aggro occurs in busy locations. Some of the criticisms of defensible space theory gives us an indication of the possible reasons for this.

Mawby (1977b), while agreeing with Bottoms' (1974) assessment that the theory is *plausible*, suggests that it is too narrow. Two deficiencies are particularly important. First, there is inadequate consideration of the role of offenders. Busy places may increase the risks of being seen but they also increase the number of potential offenders who are likely to be present. Mawby cites the evidence of his kiosk study: 'whilst visibility may protect kiosks from vandalism where it is measured relative to use, kiosks in more public situations tend to be vandalised more than secluded ones, simply because they are used more' (Mawby, 1977a). Moreover, busy places may present more opportunities for crime in the way of targets. Secondly, there is inadequate consideration of type of crime. A well-defended space may reduce the likelihood of mugging or vandalism, yet increase the possibility of another type of offence because it is regarded as secure. Mawby gives the example of gardens which may be used for the storage of goods (bicycles, toys, etc.) and thus present opportunities for casual theft.

The defensible space hypothesis has been most popularly associated with the problems of high-rise living. Large blocks of flats present an anonymous and alienating environment which breeds crime. How true is this? The evidence is decidedly ambiguous. Newman's analysis of the New York housing projects indicates that the crime rate in large high-rise blocks with slab or cruciform tower design is likely to be higher. On the other hand, Baldwin's (1975b) study of crime rates in ten different housing environments in Sheffield shows that the high-rise areas were unexceptional in the levels of residential crime. Some of the conflict may be resolved by suggesting (Mawby, 1977b) that Newman does not consider differences in *offender* rates between the projects. High-rise blocks may have more offenders because they are less desirable to the average law-abiding citizen or, in the British situation where high-rise, outside London anyway, is largely confined to the public housing sector, they may be used as a dumping ground for less-desirable tenants. Conversely Baldwin's residential crime rates may conceal the fact that high-rise developments may be more prone to certain kinds of crime (e.g. mugging and vandalism) while at the same time reducing the risks of others (burglary and residential theft). Defensible space theory provides us with a possible explanation for some of the patterns – particularly the problems associated with the space around high-rise dwellings which are neither public street nor private compound. But we should not assume too grand a role for it. As we have seen in the case of mugging (Chapter 1), precipitating opportunities provided by the environment (concealment, escape routes) must be considered in relation to the offender's knowledge of them, and of the movement of targets, not to speak of the opportunities provided by his own behaviour patterns to be in the right place at the right time. At best, defensible space theory can only be partial (Mayhew, 1979): at worst it may obscure the importance of other factors, which might nullify attempts to use the theory to control crime. We will return to this issue in Chapter 7.

Ecological Dimensions: Social Disorganisation Theories

Social disorganisation theories take a rather different perspective than opportunity theories. Essentially they are offender-orientated and stem from a view of crime based on a moral consensus of right and wrong. Shaw and McKay (1942) set their discussion of differences in delinquency rates between areas in this kind of explanatory mould, though they were more careful than some of their followers in eschewing theoretical assumptions. The major cause for high crime rates, they suggested, should be sought within areas where the normal standards of society had broken down. That is, where there was moral and physical decay, many newcomers to the city, high population densities, overcrowding, etc. The assumption is that in such conditions family structures begin to collapse and individuals are forced into a life of crime. A more specific representation of social disorganisation theory is represented by anomie. Lander (1954) in his ecological analysis of crime rates in Baltimore relies primarily on this source of explanation. Crime is a response to lack of success in matching the norms and expectations of society. Anomie, moreover, is an entirely separate dimension from socio-economic status. He concludes: 'areas characterised by instability and *anomie* are frequently the same districts which are also characterised by bad housing, low rentals and over-crowding. But the delinquency is *fundamentally* related only to the *anomie* and not to the poor socio-economic conditions of the tract.' (Lander, 1954, p. 46. his emphasis.)

Social disorganisation theories are now in some disrepute. Lander's work was criticised by Hirshi and Selvin (1967) for its failure to consider the causal order of anomie and delinquency. Is it anomie which leads to delinquency (Lander's argument) or does the failure to observe the law constitute an essential component in the definition of anomie? There is a strong case for the latter: to omit law-breaking from the set of conditions which constitute social disorganisation and artificially set it up as an outcome of the process is theoretically unjustifiable. Lander's argument becomes tautological. Social disorganisation theories should be seen as a descriptive convenience rather than a model of criminogenic behaviour. They will identify congeries of socially-relevant criteria which have an observable spatial order – poverty, poor housing, crime, etc. tend to be located in the same areas – but cannot serve as an explanation of why this is so.

Ecological Dimensions: Sub-culture Theories

The rather loose agglomeration of theories under this label was spawned by the same American tradition of the 1920s and 1930s as the social disorganisation concept. They do, however, have a sounder theoretical base though in the positivist philosophical school (see Chapter 7 for further discussion). Sub-culture theories include not only the original concepts developed by Sutherland (1939) but also the later sophistications of processes involved.

Sutherland's formulation focused on the notion that delinquency is a product of delinquents' situation in society. The law-abiding situation provides influences in the opposite direction. Glaser (1962) suggests that there are four essential elements in this process of differential association. Criminal behaviour is learned from other persons within the intimate circle of the individual: individuals encounter a mixture of legal and illegal behaviour patterns; an individual becomes delinquent when the mix of encountered behaviour favours law-breaking over law-observing; and the learning process is identical whether the behaviour is criminal or law-abiding. The last element is crucial, for it suggests that, given a bias towards criminal behaviour among associates, the individual learns to break the law in exactly the same way as in other circumstances he would learn to observe it. The ecological significance of this is that it implies (at least) the existence of neighbourhoods or areas in which the balance of behaviour encountered by the potential delinquent is in favour of violating the law. Such areas will, over time, have their delinquent bias reinforced by the process of differential association. We may legitimately ask whether we have here an explanation of the neighbourhood effect which we observed in the last chapter.

The urban environment consists of a mosaic of differing sub-cultural realms, each with its particular blend of shared perceptions, attitudes and norms in respect of the law. Some authors (Merton, 1957; Cloward and Ohlin, 1960) suggest that crime is not the only sub-culture to provide an alternative to the established order of society. Sub-cultures based on conflict and retreatism also flourish. The frustration of legitimate opportunities may be resolved through the catharsis of violence or withdrawal assisted by alcohol or drugs. Where such outlets become the norm, a sub-culture exists – a skid row is born. Alternative sub-cultures, however, need not necessarily be spatially discrete and can co-exist within a single neighbourhood.

The mechanism of association involves not just the transmission of definitions of what is or is not deviant behaviour, but also of criteria more directly relevant to future offending. First, criminal experience is transmitted by simple observation or by word-of-mouth. Experience involves knowledge of the targets or victims, the chance of success in the operation, the consequences of failure, etc. Secondly, skills are transmitted – of selecting targets, approaching or entering them, avoiding detection, etc. Lastly, communication is important – the where, how and why information without which many criminal acts simply would not take place.

Sub-culture theories are not without limitations. They have been applied most successfully to juvenile delinquency: with adult offenders many more loopholes appear. This is because of the greater spatial constraints upon juvenile criminal behaviour which we have already noted: adults are less likely to be neatly locked into particular social networks, some of the parameters of which define the sub-cultural system (Mack, 1964). Another criticism is that sub-culture theories do not cope with offence patterns. This is certainly true: many of the precipitating opportunities outlined above are not culturally transmitted. On the other hand, the mesh between sub-culture theories and predisposing opportunities can be seen to be a close one. Finally, the power of sub-culture theories varies between different types of offence. They work well for more localised offences, for example assaults and other forms of street offence, some residential crimes, etc. but are scarcely relevant to the more extreme forms of opportunist crime, on the one hand, or of professional crime on the other.

Criticisms of the Ecological Method

While we have already taken the opportunity to note criticisms of particular ecological studies and their conclusions, there are more general criticisms of the ecological methods. They fall into four categories:

(i) The Ecological Method Leads to False or Spurious Explanations of Crime. The pattern of association between crime and potential causes observed at an aggregate level of analysis may not apply to individuals. Conclusions about individuals may then be wrong or at best be simply irrelevant: this is the basis of the ecological fallacy. We have already indicated how with race and to a lesser extent social class, inferences based on patterns of simple association at the aggregate level may be found wanting, but this danger of the ecological method is quite general. There are three options available to avoid the ecological fallacy.

One is to refuse to have anything to do with aggregate data and treat with ultimate suspicion any study that does. Secondly, more powerful techniques may be developed to isolate within the aggregate correlation the individual correlation from the aggregation bias (see Hammond, 1973), thus making explicit the relations between the levels of analysis. Thirdly, the ecological conclusion is treated with scepticism until confirmed by separate individual-level conclusions (the strength of Baldwin and Bottoms' (1976) analysis of Sheffield). Regrettably too many ecological studies have ignored the options while frequently protesting awareness of the problem. At the same time, enthusiasm for factor analytic methods, which provide sophistication with resolving the difficulty, has fuelled the criticism.

(ii) Ecological Studies are Weak on Theory. This is true in different ways. The original ecologists never tried to be strong on theory, contenting themselves with detailed empirical observations (which, it should be noted, tended to contradict some of the previous theoretical formulations now in no less disrepute than some so-called ecological theories). Secondly, in accommodating the ecological fallacy, theory had to be eschewed. Alternatively, the theorising is unconvicing or confusing. Again, factor analysis does not help as its structure is not suited to theory-testing because no *a priori* assumptions about cause and effect are required. As Baldwin (1975a) points out, some factor analysts have proceeded to justify essentially contradictory theories.

(iii) Ecological Studies Lack a Dynamic Perspective. The data normally refer to a particular point in time and therefore cannot be used to illuminate the processes by which criminal acts are generated. Again true: ecological studies tend to have an undue emphasis on patterns at the expense of processes. Again, however, the bias is unnecessary as many medical epidemiological studies have successfully used similar aggregate data to trace crucial factors in the spread of a disease.

(iv) Ecological Studies Place Undue Reliance on Certain Variables (Particularly Those Derived From Population Censuses). There is too much emphasis on relatively simple demographic, social and economic indicators which themselves may have quite complex relationships to the underlying causes of crime. The fact that the peak age for offending

is in adolescence means that areas with youthful populations may have higher crime rates. But knowledge of the offender's age may only be a clue to the reasons for offending and perhaps a rather unhelpful one. The emphasis on such variables is understandable – they are more readily obtained or available on the massive scale that makes the ecological analysis possible.

In many ways these criticisms form a pretty damning indictment of the ecological approach to the study of crime. Many studies employing them have failed to make a substantive contribution to understanding crime: some indeed have been quite definitely counterproductive, contributing to a rejection of the ecological method (for example by Hood and Sparks, 1970). But before we throw the baby out with the bathwater we should recognise the weight of evidence presented in this and the previous chapters that the environmental setting of crime is important, albeit in subtle and more variable ways than the classical ecologists anticipated in the search for a general theory to explain the distribution of crime.

A Typology of Ecological Areas

Whatever the theoretical or methodological failings of the ecological approach, it has contributed significantly to the portrayal of urban neighbourhoods in terms of their crime characteristics. What follows is a somewhat eclectic typology of the urban environment. It is eclectic because of the stubborn refusal of the ecological dimensions to provide a neat frame to the classification. There are some clear distinctions, particularly between predisposing and precipitating opportunities, but also many anomalies and variants. The mix will vary from city to city. Yet in most Western cities there are certain types of area, in age, function and land-use, which can provide the student of crime with an introduction to its geographical distribution.

(i) The city centre is the primary area of precipitating opportunity. Here are concentrated the locations of a variety of offences – shoplifting, pickpocketing, criminal damage, non-residential burglary (of shops and offices), vehicle theft, minor assaults and affrays (those without residential context), etc. The opportunities are predominantly target orientated: but the attraction of city centres for legitimate activities which bring the potential offender within range of the opportunity should not be overlooked.

(ii) Industrial and commercial zones form a second type of precipitating area. Since the number of people afforded legitimate access to such areas is less than to the city centre, the level of victimisation is generally lower. Industrial zones in proximity to delinquency residence areas are likely to have a higher crime rate; this means older inner-city industrial areas where factories and workshops were often mixed in with workmen's homes. In these areas, too, premises would be smaller and less secure – more attractive to casual theft than the modern slab-sided factory segregated from housing by planning regulations. Industrial zones may also be characterised by a predisposing social environment – an acceptance of levels of pilfering and other forms of 'loss'. So little is known about the distribution of this type of often unreported theft, that indicating the sort of industrial area where it may be more prevalent is hazardous. Pointing the finger at docklands and other areas where goods are stored or transhipped rather than made may concur with popular image, but losses elsewhere may be just as serious but less likely to be notified or subject to intensive policing.

(iii) Inner-city residential areas have a high concentration of offender residences but a high proportion of offences are also committed there. These are the districts where predisposition and precipitation combine to produce the most obvious 'criminal' or 'delinquency' areas of the city: they are the areas on which the ecologists' attention has been focused over the years. Such areas may be divided into two basic subtypes which we have already found useful in describing the distribution of different types of crime. First, *residual* areas comprise inner-city districts where there is some degree of social cohesion allied with a relatively balanced demographic structure – the working-class slum, the Bethnal Greens of this world. Some of these areas are relatively crime-free but more often than not the strong traditions of neighbouring, family networks and mutual support are paralleled by equally strong traditions of petty thieving and violence, of criminal networks and rejection of the law. If sub-culture theory has any relevance it must be in this type of area and above all it is the social environment which dominates the predisposition towards crime. That so many crimes also occur in residual areas reflects on one hand the opportunities provided by a mix of land-uses but also the prevalence of petty, casual, spur-of-the-moment crimes which would not take place if opportunities were not local.

In contrast, *transitional* areas conform more to the social disorganisation or anomie models if they have any validity. Such areas have demographic structure biased towards non-family units; turnover rates of population are high; social controls are weak and anonymity characterises interpersonal relations. Crimes in these areas are, however, also opportunist, casual and petty, but unlike residual areas, much more likely to be impersonal: cheque fraud, theft from prepayment meters, drug-taking. It is one of the major weaknesses of ecological studies especially those employing factor analytical methods, that the subtle distinctions between residual and transitional areas have been so rarely recognised. For youth in the residual area, crime may be normal behaviour during adolescence; for the inhabitant of the transitional area, crime may reflect failure to achieve adequate economic or social status. In the residual area it is rarely a plea for help; in the transitional area it quite often is. It should be emphasised, however, that these differences are blurred by the fact that the same people may reside in both types of area at different stages in their life cycle. Moreover, the spatial identity of residual and transitional areas may not always be clear-cut.

The extreme form of the inner-city area is the *ghetto*. Here the social, economic and cultural bases of segregation are reinforced by overt expressions of prejudice based usually on race but sometimes on religion or ethnic origins. In the ghetto situation, intra-group offending is exaggerated: criminal behaviour is as confined as any other within the ghetto walls. Yet one must beware of equating ghettos with crime. As Chambliss (1975) shows in his discussion of the Japanese community in Seattle, ghettos can be relatively crime-free. Chambliss relates this to the fact that the Japanese have retained a balanced social structure within their community. Leadership and wealth, in relative terms, are located in proximity to the less privileged members of the community, and not as in many ghetto situations removed to some invisible milieu beyond the ghetto walls. So social cohesion and the informal social controls which accompany it are much more powerful. The effect may also emanate from strong cultural traditions retained in the ghetto – for example in the Asian immigrant communites of British cities (Bottoms, 1967). The ghetto effect, therefore, can serve to polarise the criminal environment by exaggerating in either direction the effects of certain key factors. A crime policy which misidentifies these factors or their effects is likely to be in trouble in the ghetto – a point we will return to later.

A final inner-city type is provided by *urban renewal projects*. These are becoming of increasing importance as traditional slums are pulled down and replaced. Such projects vary widely in character and in criminality. They have given rise to at least one major theory about the relations between crime and environment – defensible space theory which we have already examined. Urban renewal projects are difficult to categorise in terms of crime. In general, they have rather more crime than the average as with the other inner-city types. However it has been shown that there is wide variation in crime rates (and rates of offending) between ostensibly similar projects (cf. Baldwin, 1975b; Newman, 1972; Mawby, 1977b). These differences are not easily explained by the social composition of the projects nor, as we have seen, very adequately by the design of the physical environment. Pehaps the crucial element is again a kind of ghetto effect: the newness, the rawness, the social imbalance arising from tenant-selection policies and the architectural stereotyping combine to exaggerate the social isolation of the inhabitants. The opportunities for criminal activity are then more readily exploited. Whatever the reasons, this type of environment is associated with particular types of crime. Mawby (1977b) suggests that high-rise projects (most inner-city examples are of this type, though the trend is now for low-rise in all locations) have rather more offenders against vehicles and thefts from doorsteps (largely milk) and rather less residential burglary. My own surveys suggest that domestic violence is more prevalent in inner-city housing projects.

(iv) Suburban residential areas are as a whole much lower in both offence and offender rates. There are, however, two kinds of suburban neighbourhood which stand out in terms of crime. The more significant of these is the *public housing estate* which may suffer an incidence of crime not dissimilar to inner-city districts. It must immediately be said, however, that only one or two estates in any city will acquire the status of criminal area, the remainder will be as law-abiding as their suburban counterparts in the private housing sector. The 'rough' or 'problem' council estate has been identified in Britain (Morris, 1957; Wilson, 1963; Baldwin, 1975b; Herbert, 1979) as an older estate (usually built in the inter-war period), rather low in density, having a housing stock not always up to modern standards but comparatively low in rent. It has frequently been subject to differential house allocation policies – problem tenants have been encouraged to live there or have filtered into it as the cheap end of the council house spectrum. Typical of crimes in the problem estate are vandalism and residential theft – both burglary and stealing from dwellings and gardens. Numerically less common, but highlighting the nexus of social problems, is theft from prepayment meters by sitting tenants. As Mawby (1977b) points out, for Sheffield offence and offender rates of the problem council estate may exceed

that for the urban renewal project despite the latter's reputation as a criminogenic environment.

The second of the suburban criminal areas is the run-down, middle-class area that equates with the transitional area of the inner-city. However, the *suburban transitional area* is neither so low status nor so criminal, although it has many of the same characteristics of anonymity and transiency. Lambert (1970) identifies one such area in his sector of Birmingham – an area where there is a local concentration of residential theft, bicycle stealing and minor disputes involving neighbours. It is also the common residential area of the psychological offender, for example the middle-aged female shoplifter (see Figure 2.3: cluster of offenders north-west of city centre – the only cluster in stippled areas) or male child-molester.

The remaining areas are relatively but by no means absolutely crime-free. No part of the city is totally crime-free, though some, particularly the highest-status areas furthest from the high offender areas, have a remarkably low incidence of crime. What I think is clear at this stage is that neither the patterns of criminal areas nor the putative causes for them will yield to simplistic explanations. The motivations to crime are not just economic, nor social nor yet psychological but a complex and ever-changing amalgam. Having in a sense now exploded, constructively I hope, some of the myths surrounding reported crime rates, it is time to turn to estimates of the real level of crime and its impact on communities.

4 CRIME AND THE COMMUNITY

The fact that some parts of cities suffer much more crime than others is no news to most urban dwellers. The evidence is all too obvious: graffiti, vandalism, the armoured shop-fronts, the wail of police sirens all point to the 'criminal areas'. But to what extent do these reflect the real distribution of crime? Few of us will have been victims for crime is still a rare event so we base our perceptions on other sources than our direct experience. The last three chapters have been largely concerned with the evidence of official statistics. How does this relate to the real distribution of crime? The interrelatedness, in a community context, of myths, perceptions and realities of crime and the reactions to it are the themes of this chapter. First, however, the significance of recorded crime must be assessed to establish its relevance, if any, to a community-based understanding of crime patterns.

The Production of Official Crime Rates

Studies based on officially-recorded crime suffered a number of swingeing attacks in the 1960s and early 1970s. The basis for these attacks was the observation that the police have considerable discretion in the acceptance of an incident as violating the criminal code and in methods of identifying suspects (for example Banton, 1964; Wilson, 1968). So definitions of crime could be regarded as products of police procedures rather than of the criminal statutes. At the same time, the extent of unreported or undetected crime which evaded the sanctions of the law was being increasingly emphasised.

The criticisms followed two main perspectives. Labelling theorists (for example Becker, 1963; Matza, 1964, 1969; Lemert, 1967) focused attention on the means by which definitions of deviant behaviour are achieved by the various agents of the crime control system. Deviancy is not a quality of the act or actors but an imposition by those delegated to circumscribe it. Alternatively, deviant definitions are located in the transactions between the controllers and the controlled (see, for example, Sacks, 1972). In either event studies based on officially-recorded crime were regarded as highly suspect (Kitsuse and Cicourel, 1963). Crime rates reflect not the incidence of crime in an area but the degree of police activity which will vary according to the subjective assessments of the policeman. Hence the proposition that patterns of recorded crime are a consequence of differential policing (Wiles, 1975).

It is worth asking the question how do crimes become recorded? Mawby's study of policing in Sheffield looks at this issue in some detail (Mawby, 1979b). He makes the important distinction between the *reporting* of the incidents and the *detection* of offenders. There is no reason to suppose that these should necessarily concur. In Table 4.1 the reporting agents for his sample of indictable crimes are identified. Three

Table 4.1: Reporting Agents for Indictable Crimes: Sheffield, 1971

	%
Victim	74.6
Private law enforcer	2.8
Witness	6.4
Offender	0.7
Alarm	1.5
Police	5.3
Indirect[a]	8.7
Total (N = 676)	100.0

a. Offences admitted by the offender but not otherwise reported.
Source: Mawby (1979b), Table 4.1

out of four crimes are reported by the victim; add in reporting by witnesses and private law enforcers (who are usually employees of victims such as store detectives) and we can see that in the vast majority of cases discretion, at least initially, lies with the public and not with the police. Such findings are confirmed elsewhere in England by Bottomley and Coleman (1976) and in the United States by Reiss (1971). The police are responsible for the notification of barely one in twenty offences. The most surprising feature of these figures is the role offenders play in reporting offences. Unsolicited admissions of otherwise unreported offences are rare (0.7 per cent). However, indirect reporting by the offender is the second most important category. These are offences admitted by offenders (normally during questioning on being apprehended for other offences) *but not otherwise reported*, i.e. by the victim. Such incidents comprise nearly one-tenth of the total: typical are burglaries and thefts from vehicles involving small amounts of property or which may even have gone unnoticed by the victim.

Mawby examines variations in these proportions in high and low crime rate areas. For victim reporting he found no appreciable difference between the areas – somewhat surprising since sub-culture theory would suggest less victim reporting in high crime areas. The proportion of witnesses reporting crime varied but not consistently according to offender rate. Police reporting was found to vary considerably – from 1.8 per cent to 17.8 per cent in the nine areas studied – but not in the direction indicated by the differential policing hypothesis. More crimes were reported by the police in the low crime areas. Regrettably, Mawby omits to inform us about variations in indirect reporting.

Table 4.2 accounts for the method of clearance of offences from the same study. In fact the sample here is slightly different in that it comprises all offences committed by offenders from the nine study areas

Table 4.2: Method of Clearing Indictable Offences: Sheffield, 1971

		%
Victim		16.1
Private law enforcer		9.7
Witness		3.1
Offender gives himself up		3.1
Offender obvious		3.3
Police[a]		22.7
caught in the act	9.7	
policework	5.2	
use of discretion	6.9	
Unknown		2.4
Indirect[b]		39.6
Total (N = 578)		100.0

a. Sub-categories do not sum due to omission of unknown police detections.
b. Admitted by offender during questioning about other offences.
Source: Mawby (1979b), Tables 5.1 and 5.2.

whereas Table 4.1 covers all offences committed in the same areas. What is being scrutinised here is the method of identifying offenders. Again we find some surprises. More crimes are cleared up by the offender's own admission (usually while being questioned for other offences where he was caught in the act or where there is a weight of circumstantial evidence against him) than any other source. The police were responsible for the next largest group though nearly half these were offenders caught in the act. Police discretion was involved in 6.9 per cent of detections – most commonly the questioning of individuals acting suspiciously. Policework – questioning of suspects, etc. – only accounted for 5.2 per cent. Fingerprints were used to clear four offences (0.7 per cent)! Victims identified 16.1 per cent of offenders mainly because they knew him or her. Private law enforcers were responsible for a rather larger share of detections than reportings because most of their reports were cleared (e.g. shoplifters caught in the act). Witnesses, on the other hand, were a rather less significant source of clearance.

Area variations in detection methods are greater than for reporting, but again consistency is lacking. There are more indirect detections among residents of high crime rate areas, but little evidence that it is local crime which is cleared in this way. Police detections, however, do not differ from other direct detections in terms of rates, though more offenders tend to be caught in the act in high rate areas. Mawby also found that use of police discretion was a more common method of clearance in *low* rate areas, and if the offender was not resident in the locality. All this leads Mawby to an unequivocal conclusion:

> *It thus appears that whether we consider offence or offender data, all reported offences, all detected offences, or only police detections, there is no evidence to suggest (let alone demonstrate) that police involvement in any way creates differences in crime rates between different residential areas.* (Mawby, 1979b, p. 125, his emphasis.)

Now Mawby's data are based on recorded crimes. They do not refute the criticisms of official crime rates, but rather question their relevance. The police are involved in reporting and clearing such a small proportion of crimes that the role of the police as proactive rather than reactive must be seen to be severely restricted. The labelling perspective undoubtedly presents useful insights into the definition of crime in situations where the police do take a proactive role – the so-called victimless crimes like drug-abuse or prostitution – but for the vast majority of violence and property offences it is to the public that we must turn to understand how and why crimes enter the official record.

There is a further distinction to be made: that is between *reporting* and *recording* crimes. Not all crimes reported to the police end up in the official record. Indeed as Coleman and Bottomley (1976) indicate, the proportion of incidents written off by the police as 'no crime' may be as high as 10 per cent. There are no good studies of the incidence of 'no-criming' in cities. This is in any case a difficult area of police discretion for it encompasses a wide range of circumstances. At one extreme are genuine mistakes and false reports; in the middle some arbitrary police practices such as regarding bicycle thefts as no crime if the cycle is recovered within a few days; at the other extreme is the unwillingness of the police to become involved in domestic disputes. Some of these circumstances would warrant closer attention. However, despite the likelihood that 'no-criming' will be more common among incidents reported by the public, the extent of this practice is unlikely to disturb our emphasis on the victim's definitions of crime.

No-criming is a particular kind of non-recording – one in which a report is initially accepted as containing a criminal definition but which on investigation (or at the wishes of the complainant, etc.) is subsequently reclassified. Other reports may be initially refused by the police – because they think it malicious or lacking in criminal intent; or because they do not believe the complainant; or because there is a lack of corroborating evidence; or because they have resolved the situation to the satisfaction of the complainant (for examples of this see Black, 1970; Lambert, 1970; Reiss, 1971; Rubinstein, 1973). The credibility of complainants and police perceptions of their own role in the community may be influential factors in the recording process and both may vary between communities (Cain, 1973).

The decision to report an incident in the first place is a further source of variation; Sparks *et al.* (1977) found that the personal characteristics of victims had no bearing on their willingness to report the incident, apart from a slight tendency for females to be more likely to report than males. Differences between their three survey areas in reporting are, however, considerable. Indeed, the data from this thorough survey of victimisation in London may be used to illustrate both the extent and variation of the reporting and recording of crime (Table 4.3). After considerable effort to ensure comparability, (i.e. eliminating non-personal crimes, offences committed elsewhere, etc.), Sparks and his co-workers are able to conclude that the ratio between survey-estimated and recorded crime rates is an astonishing 11.1 : 1. The ratio varies with the type of crime – least for burglary at 4.2 : 1 and most for 'other thefts' at 48 : 1. It also varies with area. The highest ratio obtains in Hackney (14.6 : 1) – predominantly white and working-class; it is lower in Brixton (12.5 : 1), a working-class area with a substantial black minority; and least in Kensington (8.6 : 1), white and middle-class. In Table 4.3 I have taken the liberty of reinterpreting the figures from Sparks' study in order to highlight the effect of area differences in the incidence, reporting and recording of crime. To do this, an expected number of recorded incidents is generated by assuming that the rate of incidence of events does not vary between the three areas, and that in each an average proportion is reported and recorded. Of course these averages are derived from the survey data and the fre-

Table 4.3: Crime Rates, Differential Reporting and Differential Recording: London, 1972

	Crime rates (per 1000 pop. aged 18+)		Incidents recorded by police			Breakdown of difference due to area differences in:		
	Estimated by victim survey	Recorded by police	Actual No.	Expected No.[a]	Difference between actual and expected	Incidence	Reporting	Recording
All offences								
Brixton	730.7	59.6	4509	4586	- 77	+ 194	- 416	+ 145
Hackney	547.5	37.4	1955	3440	- 1485	- 756	- 31	- 698
Kensington	816.2	94.2	5127	3557	+ 1570	+ 581	+ 423	+ 566
Assault, etc.[b]								
Brixton	142.2	8.3	444	303	+ 141	+ 38	+ 3	+ 100
Hackney	128.7	4.1	175	227	- 52	- 10	+ 40	- 82
Kensington	103.3	3.5	147	235	- 88	- 43	- 30	- 15
Burglary[c]								
Brixton	98.1	20.0	1094	1602	- 508	- 345	- 331	+ 168
Hackney	133.0	13.3	570	1202	- 632	+ 76	+ 84	- 792
Kensington	152.2	59.1	2381	1242	+ 1139	+ 270	+ 246	+ 623

a. Expected number is derived by assuming that victimisation rates and the reporting and recording of incidents are average for all three areas. The variation between areas is solely due therefore to differences in population 18 years and over.

b. Includes robbery and theft from person.

c. Includes theft in dwellings.

Note: The figures given in this table are subject to the rounding errors incorporated in the source.

Source: Sparks *et al*. (1977), Tables 6.4 and 6.6, with additional calculations.

quencies generated are relative to the survey totals. Using broader city-wide or societal estimates, if these were available, would alter the values in the table but not their relationship to one another.

Hackney has the lowest recorded crime rate of the three areas but also the lowest proportion of incidents reaching the official record. Compared to what might be expected if it suffered as much crime as the other areas and reporting and recording practice were no different, Hackney has 43 per cent fewer recorded offences. About half of these are due to the fact that Hackney suffers less crime (at least as measured by the survey). Most of the remainder are due to the tendency of the police to be unwilling to record offences in Hackney. In this area, residents show little tendency to over- or under-report. In Kensington the opposite applies. This area suffers more crime than would be expected and the police record a higher proportion of reports. However, unlike Hackney, Kensington's residents are more likely to report their victimisations. In Brixton a rather different pattern emerges: the close match between expectation and actuality conceals an excess of incidence turned into a deficit by a high degree of reticence in reporting. The police in Brixton, however, largely restore the equilibrium by above average acceptance of reports.

Aside from questions of incidence these patterns raise interesting questions about the sources of the disparities. Middle-class residents of Kensington suffer more crime, are more willing to report it and are more likely to have their complaints accepted by the police (the rate of no-criming is less than the other areas – Sparks *et al.*, 1972, p. 159). The white working-class residents of Hackney tend to have their reports rejected. In the racially-mixed community, there is evidence of unwillingness to involve the police but, in a perhaps sensitive situation for the police, recording is high. The social background to the reporting and recording process seems to be clearly implicated by these patterns, even if tentatively, in view of the limited scope of the survey in terms of the types of community covered. But it is the attributes of the community and not of the individuals who reside there that we should examine: we will continue this theme a little later when we turn to attitudes to crime.

One of the conclusions of our review of patterns of recorded crime was the need for caution when examining overall crime rates. We should observe this caution again now. In Table 4.3 the rates for two important categories of offence are also given which generally confirm the overall pattern yet provide some contradictions. Assault and other offences against the person have low proportions of reporting and even lower rates of recording. Burglary is a fairly homogeneous theft group with a fairly high rate of both reporting and recording. Area differences in reporting assaults are generally weak; willingness to report in Kensington and unwillingness in Brixton focus on burglaries (and the other forms of theft not included in the table). The contrasts in recording between Hackney and Kensington are even more exaggerated for burglary, but not evident for violence. The police may thus be interpreting class-differences in terms of property. In Brixton, the police are more likely to record both assaults and burglaries.

Is there a consistent relationship between reporting and recording levels? All other things being equal, the more reporting that occurs, the less recording would be expected – on the grounds that if the reporting threshold is lower more marginal incidents will get reported which the police may decide to reject. Only Brixton fits this inverse rule. Indeed reporting thresholds are far from a monolithic concept: more crime may be reported because the victims are less tolerant of deviant activity, or define more activity as deviant, or are more reliant on the police for dealing with it, or are less afraid of involving the police, or have an insurance policy which makes claims conditional on report, etc., etc. Likewise, recording levels may be high not just because less marginal crime is brought forward, but also because the police are less disposed towards alternative remedies, or complainants are confident and articulate, or the police are concerned to be seen to be doing their job, etc. Sparks *et al.*'s London study indicates just how important are the effects of reporting and recording on crime rates. Their finding that the personal characteristics of the victim are not important puts the ball in the community's court, but the limited scope of the study in spatial terms does not allow elaboration of possible community effects. It seems that the effects are greater for property offences than violence – we found earlier that recorded rates of property offences are more differentially distributed within cities – but the extent to which disparities in the real rates are systematically exaggerated or diminished by reporting or recording practices remains to be elucidated.

Similar wide disparities in recording and reporting rates among US cities are observed by Skogan (1976). The proportion of personal and commercial robberies recorded by the police varies from 19 per cent in Milwaukee to 100 per cent in Newark. The range is slightly less but still considerable for burglary: from 22 per cent again in Milwaukee to 79 per cent in both St Louis and Miami. A strong association between the rates for these two different crimes suggests that there are general, rather than specific, factors behind the pattern. Skogan attributes the disparities to differences in police resources and professionalism, in political responsiveness and in the reward structure employed. Some of these are peculiar to the fragmented nature of the American police system, others are just as valid in the more uniform or centralised systems of police authority in Western Europe. Citizen reporting, while of the same magnitude as police recording (about the same proportion ov events are 'lost' at each stage) is much less variable – 76 per cent of robberies are reported in Miami while Portland, Oregon occupies the other extreme at 52 per cent. For burglary, Miami is again highest with 67 per cent – a figure shared by Cincinnati – whereas Houston is lowest with 51 per cent. There is no consistent pattern of association between reporting and recording among the cities, though the National Research Council (1976), using the same source, reports an *inverse* relationship between survey-reported and official crime rates for aggravated assault.

So the production of official crime rates has a very real bearing on understanding patterns of crime. A proactive role for the police, if it is important at all, is very limited in its scope. Differential policing is thus largely irrelevant. Differential recording is not, for the police have the ability to apply massive, if passive, discretion in reacting to reports brought forward by members of the public. Differential reporting is just as important a source of disparity and more fundamental since it is the initial discretion in the chain between the act and its consequences.

Patterns of Victimisation

The victims of crime, like the events themselves and the offenders, are far from randomly distributed in the population. Some types of individual are much more likely to become victims than others. Moreover, unlike lightning, victimisation has a tendency to strike twice (or more) in the same place. Where you live, as well as who you are, affects your chances, but perhaps most important the sorts of situations into which your lifestyle takes you determines victimisation risks. As with other ways of defining the incidence of crime, there are severe measurement problems in ascertaining victimisation rates (reviewed by Sparks *et al.*, 1977, Chapter 3). Victims may suffer problems of recall, especially if the event was not recent; victims may be inhibited in recounting certain types of events, e.g. an act of violence by somebody they know; they may be inarticulate or hostile to the interviewer; they may have varying opinions about what constitutes criminal behaviour or simply not perceive the act in any way unusual. One may end up agreeing with Cicourel (1976) that there is no such thing as a 'real' crime rate: merely a multiplicity of truths which can be lumped together. The more successful victimisation surveys, through the exercise of considerable care, have eliminated much of the bias (for example Hindelang, 1976; Skogan, 1976; Sparks *et al.*, 1977). Yet there remains much ground for scepticism about the levels of crime revealed. Victimisation studies have value in the internal relativities they reveal, but rather less credibility should be invested in absolute rates or in numerical comparisons between surveys.

(a) The Risks of Victimisation

(i) Sex and Marital Condition. In general males are more likely to be crime victims than females. Hindelang, *et al.*, (1978) give a ratio of 1.5 for a survey of eight American cities. In London the margin is smaller – 48.8 per cent of males and 42.6 per cent of females suffering at least one victimisation during the preceding year (Sparks *et al.*, 1977). The tendency among American respondents of the single/widowed/divorced to suffer more crime is not replicated among London respondents. Violent crimes are more likely to have male victims (with the exception of rape); for property offences distinctions are less clear cut. Males are more likely to be injured in offences against the person and suffer loss in offences against property.

(ii) Age. Almost universally, victimisation surveys report an inverse relationship between age and the risks of crime. Table 4.4 illustrates the variations in Hindelang *et al.*'s (1978) American data. The highest risks are in the 16-19 years age-group and decline regularly as age increases. The pattern of lower risks for the elderly is consistent for the three types of personal victimisation considered by Hindelang but the decline is a good deal less dramatic for violence with theft, and theft without injury. Conklin (1976) reports that robbery is, in fact, more prevalent among the elderly in Boston (Table 4.5). However the differences are due to the risks of purse-snatch or robbery in the home among the elderly – an indication of the importance of situational factors in accounting for age differentials. In relative terms Table 4.4 indicates that older victims tend to suffer property-only offences.

In a study of Sheffield, Mawby (1979a) indicates that juvenile victimisation is less clearly differentiated than adult whether by area or status. For juveniles, the nature of the victim's relations with offenders

Table 4.4: Estimated Personal Victimisation Rates by Age: US Cities, 1973

Rates per 1000 relevant population	12-15	16-19	20-24	Aged 25-34	35-49	50-64	65+	Total
Assaultive violence:								
with theft	7	8	6	5	6	6	4	6
without theft	54	76	58	37	18	11	6	32
Personal theft without injury	26	29	23	20	21	21	19	22
Total	87	114	87	62	45	38	29	60

Source: Hindelang *et al*., (1978), Table 1.1.

Table 4.5: Reported Robbery[a] Victimisation Rates by Age: Boston, 1968

	Rates per 10,000 relevant population		
	Aged under 60	60+ years	Total
Street robberies (excluding purse-snatch)	4.4	4.4	4.4
Purse-snatch	1.0	3.7	1.5
Robberies in the home	0.8	2.4	1.0
All individual robberies	6.2	10.5	6.9

a. Individual robberies only.
Source: Conklin (1976), derived from Tables 10.1 and 10.2

is more important than the surrounding environment. For adults in Sheffield a clear relationship emerged between risks of victimisation and the offender rate of areas. So not only do the risks vary with age but also the significance of particular aspects of background and circumstances.

(iii) Social Class and Income. Findings on this issue have been far from straighttorward. Sparks *et al.* (1977) found no consistent differences between the classes in reporting offences against the person or burglary. The US National Crime Surveys (Hindelang, 1976) suggested that risks of personal victimisations were higher among low income groups and of property victimisations among higher income families. Hindelang *et al.* (1978) indicate that the seriousness of the offences declines with income, with the exception of rich young blacks who suffer more serious victimisations than their white counterparts. Risk of assault is greater at the extremes of the income range and low for middle income families. In Scandinavia, however, low status individuals had a lower risk of violence than members of the middle and high status groups (Wolf and Hauge, 1975).

(iv) Race. There is a large measure of agreement that non-whites are more likely to be victims of crime than whites in both the US and Britain, but this broad rule contains some exceptions. So, while in London 33 per cent of blacks reported one or more incidents of violence and only 11 per cent of whites did so (Sparks *et al.*, 1977), in the United States Hindelang *et al.* (1978) show that as far as assaults *without theft* are concerned the risks for whites are higher. Patterns of victimisation are, however, consistently intra-racial. It is with race that

measurement problems may be most severe, since cultural differences may exaggerate response biases, for example those arising from varying definitions of crime. We have, moreover, already noted that, in Britain certainly, non-whites are far from a homogeneous group and the patterns of recorded crime show considerable variation between the racial sub-groups. Patterns of victimisation are likely to be similarly varied though not necessarily in the same way as those recorded by the police.

(v) Social Activity. A number of studies have implicated the degree of social activity in victimisation risks. For example, in their study of a New York ghetto community Kleinman and David (1973) postulated that victimisation is linked to visibility and contact with others in the community. They found that long-term residents, members of community organisations and persons who had been offered stolen goods were all more likely to be victims. Church-goers and people with relatives in the area (which might also contribute to visibility) were found to have no effect on risks. Frequency of social activities outside the home is correlated with risks (the more nights out the higher the risk) but curiously neither the location nor type of activity are good predictors of differences (Sparks *et al.*, 1977).

(vi) Multiple Victimisation. There is widespread recognition that the risk of being a victim of crime on more than one occasion is greater than that yielded by a random distribution. Sparks *et al.* (1977) found that there were 11 per cent more people suffering two or more victimisations than would be expected from a random model based on the Poisson distribution. The pattern holds for all three of their survey areas and for both property and violence offences, although repeated victimisations are as a whole less common for violence. Similar conclusions are reached by Hindelang *et al.* (1978) who suggest that some individuals are victimisation-prone – by virtue of their possession of precipitating attributes such as carelessness, foolhardiness or provocativeness, or predisposing attributes such as affluence, isolation, or frequenting the haunts of offenders whether deliberately or accidentally. The importance of this last factor is indicated by a significantly higher proportion of victimisations by non-strangers among multiple victims. There is also some evidence that multiple victims are more common among those who admit to the commission of offences, particularly violence (Sparks *et al.*, 1977). A number of hypotheses have been put forward to explain the differential distribution of multiple victim-

isation. Reinforcement or contagion suggests that victims modify their behaviour in the light of their experience or they become 'marked' as an easy victim. Heterogeneity assumes that risks vary *between* sub-groups of the population (as by sex, age or class) but that randomness occurs *within* the sub-groups. Cumulation involves the multiplication of risks according to the particular characteristics of the individual. Reinforcement/contagion is extremely difficult to test with standard cross-sectional data, but the fact that multiple victimisations do not regularly involve the same type of offence makes this explanation unlikely. Heterogeneity is favoured by Sparks *et al.* (1977) though somewhat cautiously. It is largely rejected by Aromaa (1974) for violence victims (at least as far as area of residence, sex, age and marital condition are concerned) in favour of cumulation.

(b) Environmental Factors in Victimisation

The extent to which situational factors are important in the distribution of crime has already been discussed in Chapter 1 from reported statistics. The evidence from victimisation studies is a good deal scarcer but it points in the same direction. The chances of victimisation and the nature of the experience (and its consequences as we shall later see) are intimately connected with the setting within which it occurs. On one level the connection is direct and obvious: shoplifting occurs in shops, burglaries in buildings, etc. so being a truck-driver does rather foreclose on the risks of being a victim of shoplifting. However, on a rather different level, the connections are much more interesting, for the properties of the place where the crime takes place have repercussions on the degree of loss or injury sustained, and thus on the seriousness of the crime, on the trauma suffered and on the reactions of the victim (and other parties concerned). The pre-eminent property of the scene of the crime is its privacy; of secondary importance is familiarity (to the victim). We cannot, however, observe these effects for crime as a whole because of the normative role of place in particular types of crime, for example shoplifting. Rather than attempting to be comprehensive, three examples have been selected – assault, robbery and burglary – and embedded in a more general discussion of the violence and property groups.

(i) Micro-environments of Violence. Hindelang *et al.* (1978) present some very general evidence of differences in the likelihood of injury according to the situation of personal victimisations (see also Gottfredson and Hindelang, 1976). Victims are most likely to be injured in their

own home, least likely in commercial buildings or a public conveyance (Table 4.6). These are at the extremes of the privacy and familiarity scales. Why should a victim suffer more if attacked in his own castle?

Table 4.6: Micro-environment of Loss or Injury: United States, 1973

Location	% of personal victimisations resulting in[a]	
	Injury	Loss of property
Office	25*	9
School	25*	20
In victim's home	32	25
Near victim's home	25*	31
On street	25*	34
Commercial buildings or public conveyance	18	43
All incidents	25	32

a. Assaults and thefts involving personal confrontation.
*Approximation only given in source.
Source: Hindelang *et al*. (1978).

The key is the anonymity of the assailant. Violence in the home is more likely to involve non-strangers than elsewhere – the domestic affray to use the euphemism for this kind of violence. People who are beaten up by somebody they know are less likely to report the incident, certainly to the police, perhaps even to the scrupulous interviewer (Gelles, 1979). The consequence is a spurious inflation of the seriousness of domestic violence (as evidenced by the injury suffered). What is really happening is the concealment of a great deal of violence in the home that would be revealed had it occurred in less private and familiar surroundings. In a survey of Minneapolis, none of the 57 survey-reported incidents involving members of the family had been reported to the police (Reynolds, 1973).

On the other hand, attacks by strangers in the home may produce a diversity of reactions among victims because of the perceived affront. At one extreme the response may be physical force; at the other shocked immobilisation. According to Hindelang *et al*. (1978), both reactions are associated with higher risks of injury, though this is complicated by the type of weapon used by the assailant. What the victim should do – remain calm, offer no physical or verbal attack on the assailant, but show no extreme of fear or shock – is what the domestic victim finds most difficult. In this case the higher proportion of injuries suffered in the home may truly reflect a more serious level of violence being offered by intruders in the home. Whether the violence is a response to physical resistance by the victim or whether it occurs in anticipation of such resistance remains unresolved.

What Hindelang *et al*'s. analysis fails to do is to distinguish adequately two very different forms of violence – impulsive and purposive. Impulsive violence is a product of the moment and its circumstances, though its roots may lie in the past. Violence is purposive when it is entailed to achieve other ends, usually theft. Aggravated assaults (US) or assaults occasioning grievous bodily harm (UK) are in the main impulsive. The violence of robbery is largely purposive (Block, 1977).

With robbery, the setting of the incident is less significant than other situational factors with respect to the consequences for the victim. In an analysis of robbery in Chicago, Block (1977) suggests that the use of a gun, the use (or threat) of force and the resistance offered by the victim are the most powerful determinants of the success of the robbery and of the likelihood of injury to the victim. Use of force is less likely when a gun is used. The victim runs much greater risk of injury if resistance is offered when either a gun or force or especially both are being used. The location of the incident appears to have little effect on these relationships probably because the proportion of strangers perpetrating robberies is very high in all locations.

Where location may be important is in the initial level of violence offered. Dunn (1976b) finds that the privateness of the location is related to the seriousness of the means of threat used (not necessarily of the actual violence). In more public, outdoor locations, less serious means are more often used compared to indoor commercial locations where use of knives and guns predominates (see Figure 4.1). This trend is, however, reversed in the small number of robberies in private residences where the pattern is similar to outdoor locations. These relationships are much stronger for neighbourhoods with a low risk of burglary; likewise robberies in high socio-economic status areas attract a threat of greater violence. Publicness/privateness is therefore important but so also is the familiarity of the offender with the robbery location especially in relation to his perception of how familiar the potential victim is likely to be. These findings for robbery are quite the reverse for aggravated assault (Dunn, 1976a, 1976b), where the means of force offered is more serious in areas of low socio-economic status or high assault rates.

Violence is thus far from a uniform category of crime. The seriousness of impulsive violence seems related to the visibility of its location – greater violence in privacy – though this may be falsely produced

Figure 4.1: Robbery Location and Seriousness of Threat Offered: Westchester County, New York, 1970

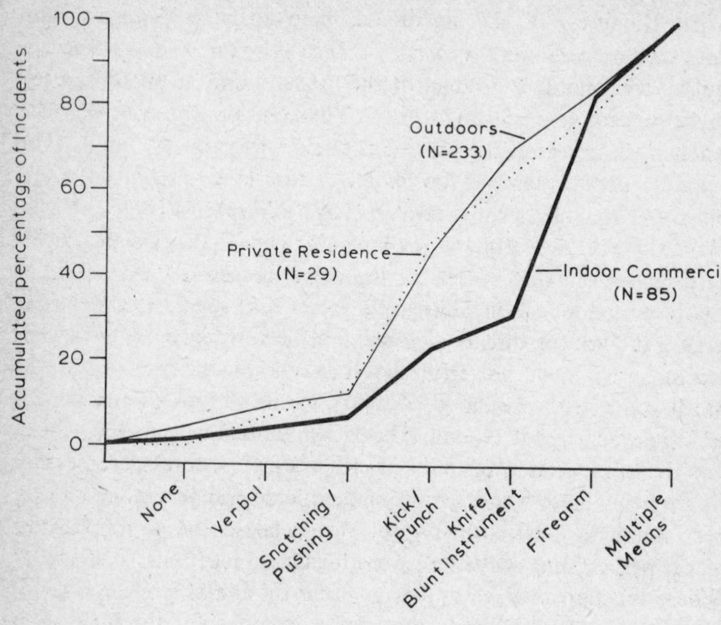

Source: Adapted from Dunn (1976b), Table 11.

by reporting and recording practices which ensure that only the most serious incidents in private become visible. Purposive violence, on the other hand, is likely to be more serious in locations unfamiliar to the offender or where he anticipates confrontation with his victim. Micro-environments of violence provide a subtle blend of privacy, anonymity, familiarity and visibility for both offender and victim, for their interaction and for the outcome of the incident.

(ii) Micro-environments of Property Victimisation. In Hindelang *et al*'s. (1978) survey of personal victimisation in the United States, 32 per cent of the respondents lost some property (theft was attempted in a further 11 per cent). In 57 per cent of the cases involving loss, the loss was less than $50. In Table 4.6 the incidence of loss is noted for various locations of the incident. Again we can observe that familiarity of the victim with the scene of the crime is important, but effect for

likelihood of loss is the reverse of that for injury. Loss is more likely in less familiar surroundings. Again also offender/victim relations are implicated. Property loss resulted in 39 per cent of incidents involving strangers, but only 11 per cent of those involving non-strangers. These figures contrast with 23 per cent of stranger-victimisations resulting in injury compared to 35 per cent non-stranger. In other ways, too, loss and injury are inversely related – for example, use of menacing weapons is connected with greater loss but less injury.

Turning now to look at the particular case of burglary, Waller and Okihiro (1978) in a study of burglary victimisation in Toronto, found it useful to separate the analyses of houses and apartments. The independent effects of surveillability, income, social cohesion and nearness to public housing on victimisation were tested using multiple regression techniques. The hypotheses were generated basically from defensible space theory. For the houses, nearness to public housing was found to be the best predictor of victimisation and income and surveillability were also important. Social cohesion was found to have no independent effect, but the hours a property was left vacant did. So people with high risks of victimisation, for example in proximity to public housing, can diminish the chance of burglary by not leaving the house unoccupied for long and by allowing it to be overlooked. For apartments, affluence was again important, but carelessness in leaving doors insecure was more important than other locational variables (a connection with the proximity of industrial premises was rejected as spurious since almost all the apartments with doormen were thus situated and none of them were victimised). Waller and Okihiro are very cautious about the validity of defensible space theory.

My own survey of burglary (Davidson, 1980b) in Christchurch, New Zealand was based on reported incidents and therefore suffers from a lack of comparison with non-victimised households. Yet bearing in mind that burglary has a rather higher-than-average reporting rate, there are some patterns of relevance to the incidence of this particular crime. These revolve round the value of goods stolen. The variability of loss was so great among all types and situations of burglary that no rationale appears to exist in the selection of burglary victims at least as far as gain is concerned. Victims in the poorest parts of the city are likely to have as much stolen as those in the richer neighbourhoods – a pattern which contradicts Waller and Okihiro's finding on affluence, though my inference is from the median neighbourhood income rather than the more reliable household income which they use. Burglary victims in Christchurch are overwhelmingly concentrated in the least wealthy districts. The poorest quarter of the city's census tracts suffered 66.4 burglaries per 1,000 households compared to the richest quarter's 12.8; 50.6 per cent of burglaries were located in the poorest quarter and these comprised 46.6 per cent of the dollar loss; 17 per cent of the thieves stole nothing; in 67.3 per cent of incidents the thief did not have to use force to gain entry and even where he did the average dollar loss was only slightly, but not significantly, greater. On none of these criteria were types of neighbourhood by income differentiated. The conclusion from the evidence was that, in Christchurch anyway, burglary is a highly opportunist criminal activity and its incidence is closely tied to the neighbourhoods where the burglars reside. On the micro-scale, vulnerability – leaving dwellings empty and/or insecure – may be the key. This finding concurs with Waller and Okihiro's on occupancy and carelessness and with Reppetto's (1974) assertion about high-risk areas in Boston.

While we have concentrated largely on burglary, there are clear indications from our discussion in Chapter 1, though few substantive studies, that micro-locational factors are important not just in the incidence but in the nature of victimisation of other types of property loss. The work of Ley and Cybriwsky (1974) on car-stripping may be cited, but shoplifting, car and cycle theft, pilfering, etc. may be fruitful areas for micro-locational enquiry.

(c) The Neighbourhood Effect in Victimisation

Earlier we noted that there were good reasons to suggest that neighbourhood variables have a strong but independent effect on offence and offender rates. Is the same true of patterns of victimisation? One good study of Chicago indicates that it is. Johnstone (1978) examines the incidence of various types of offending, arrest rates and victimisation rates from a self-report survey caried out in a sample of 221 census tracts. His objective was to test the relative effects of two aspects of 'social location' – area status and family status. He finds that of the nine indices, his victimisation index is best fitted to an area status model of the patterns. However, an even better fit is provided by a model which predicts joint additive effects of area and family with area status dominant. Table 4.7 summarises the pattern which he found (note that his index of victimisation is not a victimisation rate, nor a risk of being victimised, but a points-score based on the number of incidents reported regardless of the type or seriousness). Whatever it measures, this index increases towards the low end of the scale for both area and family status and the disparities are slightly greater

Table 4.7: Victimisation – Effects of Area Status and Family Status: Chicago, 1972

Index of victimisation[a]

		Family status			
		Low	Medium	High	Average
Area status	Low	.94	.92	.62	.90
	Medium	.86	.66	.53	.68
	High	.60	.47	.62	.57
	Average	.87	.69	.59	.71

a. Sample of 14-18 year-olds (N=1237) asked whether ever a victim of aggravated assault, burglary, larceny or robbery. Each victim given one point for each *type* of victimisation suffered. Index of victimisation is the average points per victim. See source for fuller discussion.
Source: Johnstone (1978), Table 4.

for area.

In a study of Haifa, Fishman (1979) partitions victimisation into personal, property and economic offences (the latter includes tax evasion, fraud, etc.) Victims of crimes against the person are over-represented in 'deteriorated' neighbourhoods, victims of economic offences in 'good' neighbourhoods, and those of property offences equally distributed. Patterns of multiple victimisation tend to reinforce these area differences, especially for crimes against the person.

All this lends weight to Hindelang *et al.*'s (1978) conclusion that ecological variables are important. Where you live influences the likelihood of victimisation. Such a conclusion is also implicit in the opportunity theory of crime commission. If victims are chosen not because of the opportunities they present but because the opportunity is visible to potential offenders, then proximity to the behavioural world of offenders will be important. In Christchurch, New Zealand, 32 per cent of burglary victims and 30 per cent of known burglars lived in the same small area in which resided not quite 10 per cent of the city's population (Davidson, 1980b). Other factors, too, lead towards this nexus of proximity: the high proportion of offenders familiar with their victim, especially in violence offences; the non-random distribution of the risks of multiple victimisation; and the greater than expected proportions of events with both offender and victim in the same age, sex or racial group (Hindelang *et al.*, 1978).

Situational factors are therefore implicated in patterns of victimisation at two quite distinct levels. Micro-environmental factors have a bearing on the nature but more importantly on the real or apparent seriousness of the crime. At the community level, the kind of neighbourhood and its location in relation to other types of neighbourhood are instrumental.

Perceptions of Crime

Crime is a topic which arouses strong feelings in most people yet is one of which few have direct experience. Opinions expressed in the ballot box on issues of law and order are therefore based on perceptions of crime from information which is at best second-hand. The media, public pronouncements, conversations in bars, over garden fences, at dinner tables and teabreaks, and observations of police activities and perhaps crimes are the major sources of information. Yet the issue of law and order is felt by many to be one of the most serious problems facing society. The question to be addressed here is the content and accuracy of individual perceptions of crime in relation to residential locality. Specifically, we may ask what residents know about the extent and seriousness of crime in their community, who commits it and what effect they think it has on people's activities. Just asking these questions is fraught with difficulties since in the absence of objective personal experience respondents are more likely to be swayed by the phraseology used. Asked what their chances of being burgled are, 27 per cent of the residents of the least-burgled neighbourhood of Minneapolis replied more than 50:50. Their chances (according to the official rate) were 1:1406 (McPherson, 1978). We must, as ever, emphasise relativities.

(a) How Much Crime in Your Neighbourhood?

The almost universal response to this sort of question is the same or less than elsewhere. In London, 47 per cent said the same, 40 per cent said less and 13 per cent said more (Sparks *et al.*, 1977). In the United States, in response to questions about the increase in crime, 47 per cent of respondents thought that crime had increased locally, but 86 per cent thought it had nationally (Hindelang *et al.*, 1978; see Table 4.8). Broadly speaking there is an accordance between the incidence and perception of crime. Residents of neighbourhoods with more (recorded) crime are less likely to perceive the local rate as lower than elsewhere. But even in high rate areas, the proportion who perceive the local rate as lower can still be considerable – for example, Conklin (1971) reports 53 per cent of his urban sample responding thus compared to 87 per

Table 4.8: Perceptions of Crime – Effect of Victimisation: Eight US Cities, 1973

		None	Number of personal victimisations 1	2+
		%	%	%
Has crime in the US increased?	Yes	86	87	87
Has crime in your neighbourhood increased?	Yes	46	59	66
Is your neighbourhood more or less dangerous than others?	More	6	13	16
	Average	43	46	43
	Less	51	41	41
Who commits neighbourhood crime?	Outsiders	44	42	42
	Locals	21	31	36
	Both equally	9	10	10
	Dont' know	26	17	12
People's activities are limited by fears of crime?	In general	83	85	86
	In neighbourhood	59	66	67
	Respondent	45	54	56

Source: Hindelang *et al*., (1978), Table 7.4.

cent of his suburban residents. So crime is perceived predominantly as a non-local issue.

(b) How Serious is Crime?

Perceptions of the risk of victimisation invariably overestimate the risks. Again, however, the disparity holds for different types of neighbourhood. McPhersòn (1978) finds in Minneapolis a good correlation between perceptions of risks and recorded rates for a variety of offences, though such is the gap between the perceptions and rates that her analysis must be a little suspect. On the question of neighbourhood danger, one's own neighbourhood is felt to be less dangerous than elsewhere (Hindelang *et al*., 1978; see Table 4.8). So most people, while tending to overestimate the risks, see crime as more likely to affect others than themselves. Boggs (1971) reports that central city residents tend to have rather different expectations about the type of crime that is committed in their neighbourhood: more personal violence and 'street-crimes'. On the other hand, in the inner-city areas of London covered by Sparks *et al.* (1977), burglary was well ahead of other types of crime mentioned as being committed in the neighbourhood. However, perceptions about particular offences seem much more closely connected with specific fears and concerns than the overall response to crime – a point we will return to shortly when considering fears.

(c) Who Commits Crime?

The general response seems to be someone else: the perception that crime in our neighbourhood is committed by outsiders. In US cities (see Table 4.8) nearly half the respondents pointed the finger at outsiders (Hindelang *et al.*, 1978). In Boston, Conklin (1975) shows that such opinions are held even in high crime rate areas. Even when this perception is clearly at variance with reality, people believe that the crime in their neighbourhood is committed by people coming in (Montgomery, 1973). So widespread are these beliefs, that we must consider outsider theory as fundamental to community responses to crime.

(d) Individual Versus Community Perceptions

What underpins these strong perceptions of crime as a non-local, non-personal issue? It might be expected that the experience of victimisation would affect the individual's perceptions. This appears not to be the case, though with some qualification. In Table 4.8 the opinions of victims and non-victims are compared. First, there are virtually no differences between multiple and one-time victims. Secondly, while victims are slightly less ready to perceive crime as a non-local issue, the discrepancies are still considerable. As Hindelang *et al.* (1978) remarks, the victimisation experience seems to improve knowledge without affecting general ideas: for example the perception that crime is committed by locals is improved at the expense of the 'don't-knows' in Table 4.8. Victimisation is in many ways so contradictory to general beliefs – it is personal, traumatic and often committed by non-strangers – that a conflict is set up which is resolved by rationalising the experience in terms of its rarity and randomness ('I was unlucky') while leaving one's general perception unimpeached. Three-or-more-time victims still adhere to the worse-elsewhere beliefs (Sparks *et al.*, 1977).

Other factors, race, sex, age, income, etc. have equally marginal effects on the pattern of general beliefs (Conklin, 1975; Sparks *et al.*, 1977; Hindelang *et al.*, 1978). Indeed Conklin (1975) is led to emphasise that:

> . . . *differences between communities in perceptions of crime hold even when people of similar characteristics are compared*, again suggesting that a unique criminal environment exists in each community. (pp. 80-1)

While agreeing in broad terms with the lack of effect of personal variables, Sparks *et al*. (1977) did find that the individual's evaluation of his local neighbourhood was correlated to perceptions of crime. People with negative or disapproving views of the neighbourhood were much more likely to perceive more crime in the area. It seems clear that general perceptions of crime owe more to the social environment than to the personal attributes of individuals. This has important repercussions on policy matters (see Chapter 7).

Fears of Crime

Fear of crime should not be equated with the perception of crime as a serious problem. There may be some association between the two: Conklin (1975) suggests that perceptions are inversely related to feelings of safety but only among high crime rate areas. Fears of crime tend to be high in such areas but they may also be high in some low crime areas, for example high status suburban areas (Reppetto, 1974). Indeed we may be observing here a distinction which Kleinman and David (1973) suggest is important: between the cognitive and affective aspects of opinions on crime, that is between *concern* (which directs perceptions) and *fear* (which directs actions). We have seen that the former is rooted in the community and predicated by community norms of response to the issues of crime. The latter is controlled by individual needs, particularly those emerging from anticipations of the consequences of victimisation. Those who have more to lose are more afraid as are those who are (or perceive themselves to be) less able to protect themselves. Middle-class suburban residents may acknowledge low local crime rates but still be sufficiently afraid to protect their homes from burglary. Old people may, through fear, severely curtail their activities in certain places, or at certain times of the day, in order to minimise their risk of attack, even though objectively the risk is low (Gubrium, 1974). There is little evidence that taking security precautions reduces fear, certainly among the elderly (Sundeen and Mathieu, 1976).

One factor which may be relevant is the tendency to externalise fears as well as perceptions. People on the whole feel that their activities are less limited by fears of crime than others are. And they think their neighbours less affected by fears of crime than people elsewhere (Table 4.8). Fear of crime may thus be fear of outsiders, and so exist even when at variance with reality. The extent to which the discovery that crime is located within the community causes anxiety and confusion is illustrated by Poveda's (1972) study of a small Californian industrial town.

Just why this should be so is difficult to unravel. There seems agreement that victimisation experience has no effect on general fears of crime though it may impinge on the employment of avoidance techniques by individuals (Table 4.8). A key factor is the individual's attitudes and feelings for the community. The less attachment to, or more negative feelings people have about their neighbourhood, the greater their fears of crime (Boggs, 1971; Conklin, 1971; Sparks *et al.*, 1977; Hartnagel, 1979). And yet measures of neighbourhood cohesion and social solidarity are not always related to fears of crime. Conklin (1971) and Hartnagel (1979) suggest a threshold effect to explain this: it is only in high crime areas that fears of crime are connected with lack of interpersonal trust. This issue is complicated by the interaction between fear and trust. People may fear more because of lack of trust generated by other things not connected with crime – anonymity, isolation, lack of privacy, immobility, etc. – or trust may be reduced as a consequence of fear making people retreat and take risk-avoiding measures which reduce their contact with others.

Fears of crime should be conceived as focused on two distinct levels. One is an expression of personal vulnerability in which perceived risks are matched to potential consequences. The other is related to wider concerns (crime is but one) about the quality of life against decline in which the community is seen to be a first line of defence. The interaction between fear as vulnerability and fear as community concern may explain why fears may be exaggerated while crime is seen as something that affects others (Garofalo and Laub, 1978). We should bear in mind also that fears of crime may be unrealistic but none the less real.

Attitudes to Crime and Support for the Law

Differences between areas in attitudes to crime are implicit in most of the classical ecological theories of crime. My purpose here is not to observe attitudinal elements of sub-culture as they affect offending, but to examine more generally their relationship to perceptions and fears of crime. The key factor is tolerance of criminal behaviour but we must take some care in defining what we mean by this. It may refer to attitudes towards the act itself, or towards the consequences of the act (for the offender) or indeed to the reaction of the victim (e.g. whether or not to report it). Tolerance here is taken to refer to definitions of the act (whether or not it is regarded as crime). Punitiveness will describe attitudes towards the consequences though this vastly over-simplifies the issue; and willingness to report crimes is taken as the basic criterion of support for the law.

There appears to be some degree of consensus about what constitutes a crime, particularly as far as ratings of seriousness go (Durant *et al.*, 1972; Rossi *et al.*, 1974). To be fair this assertion ought to be rephrased slightly: there appear to be few consistent differences between sex, age, race and class groups in their tolerance of deviant acts, though there remain considerable variations within sub-groups. Middle-class people tend to be more tolerant towards social disorder offences and less towards minor violence and property offences. The experience of victimisation also proves to have a less dramatic effect on tolerance than might be expected. One-time victims in London rated a series of hypothetical crimes more serious than non-victims but more serious also than multiple victims (Sparks *et al.*, 1977).

John Conklin's study of two contrasting areas of Boston provides some insight into variations in tolerance, punitiveness and support for the law at community level (Conklin, 1975). He found that there was no difference between the low crime suburban area and the high crime inner-city area in terms of their ranking of the seriousness of a set of offences. There was less agreement about whether crimes should be punished, particularly on the question of some marginal crimes such as marijuana use and gambling. Residents of the high crime area were more opposed to the suggestion that the law might be violated under certain conditions, but this difference was entirely explained by the greater authoritarianism expressed by these residents. Differences between the two communities were even greater in terms of willingness to report incidents to the police. Residents of the high crime area were much less supportive of the law, irrespective of other attitudes or other social background variables. Indeed there appears to be a strong inverse relationship between perception of crime and support for the law that holds for individuals and among communities. Those who perceive more crime are less willing to report it.

Similar conclusions are reached with respect to juvenile delinquency by Maccoby *et al.* (1958) and Hackler *et al.* (1974). In view of the multiplicity of reasons for not reporting, such consistency is notable, though as we noted earlier, far from monolithic. It is also not clear how perceptions and attitudes affect each other. Does a perception of more crime lead to a view that the police are ineffective and reporting less worthwhile? Or does a lack of support for the law lead to a lowering of police morale and heightened perceptions? Possibly both work in a vicious circle. Certainly it is unwise to ignore the role of the police since *police* perceptions of community attitudes may be instrumental in how a community's crime is dealt with (Cain, 1973).

The Role of the Community

To this point in this chapter we have eschewed attempts to integrate the various patterns we have found. Risks, perceptions, fears and attitudes are in a dynamic relationship which determines the social reaction to crime which in turn acts as a reference frame for individual reactions without which there would be little crime. The community plays an important role in this process in that it locates the social reaction and provides the key for individual response. This chapter began with some observations on how official crime rates are produced: it is to be concluded by outlining four models of the role of community as the base for social reaction.

(a) The Normative Community

This model is based on the Durkheimian notion that crime is necessary, even good, for the community. Crime increases social solidarity through its threat to the collective conscience. The community is the respository for the norms of reaction – the rules which mediate the response of a victim to the circumstances of his victimisation. In a sense the norms encapsulate the accumulated experience of what is acceptable for the collective good. It has been suggested that the norms fall in two groups (Mizruchi and Perrucci, 1962): prescriptive norms that define what should be done (for example calling the police if attacked and robbed in the street); and proscriptive norms defining what is unacceptable.

If it is accepted that norms are not uniform everywhere, then the concept of the normative community can explain why perceptions and fears of crime, support for the law, etc., have rather different properties in different communities. One community may be highly integrated, with a great deal of social interaction, rely on informal means of social control and have rather low fears of crime. Another may be characterised by anonymity, isolation, great fears, and excessive expectations of the police as agents of control. Communities with weak or non-existent norms are likely to suffer more crime and this builds a vicious circle through heightened perceptions and fears to yet more crime.

The concept of the normative community fails, however, to cope with some features of the patterns we have observed. Even within a single community norms may conflict to the point of denying their validity as arbiters of behaviour. For example proscriptions against theft may conflict with prescriptions for peer status acquisition (proving oneself by stealing) among the critical adolescent age group. The question is which norm is stronger not the absence or weakness of norms. There is conflict also between norms relating to self and norms relating to others. What goes for self may be unacceptable in others, for example expectations about drunkenness. Individuals may believe they are better able than others to cope with an excess of alcohol, looking after their property, or whatever. The normative community is therefore at best a partial model; its value is in the emphasis placed on relations between individual and group.

(b) The Supportive Community

This model is primarily concerned with relations between groups. We have noted a general belief among people that their own community is safer and more crime-free than others. Conklin (1975) suggests that beliefs in criminals as outsiders provides a mechanism for externalising fears of crime, of explaining away the need for socially and economically costly precautions. In communities with low crime rates, such a rationale is convenient and easy. In a high crime area where precautions are likely to be severely restrictive and perhaps impossible to afford, outsider theory becomes a necessary coping mechanism. The corollary of locating the general 'danger' *outside* the community is the belief that the community provides support for the individual's response to the threat.

There are two major influences on the degree of support provided by the community. First, support is strengthened by social solidarity – by strong positive feelings about the community, by well-developed social networks, by shared norms in a variety of arenas. It is weakened by social segregation, since the more homogeneous the community the narrower and more unstable is its base. Contrasts between communities also facilitate the location of external threats and may arouse greater fears especially where the contrast occurs in close proximity. Fears may become grossly exaggerated in highly segregated, homogeneous communities where social interaction is severely restricted by age, or child-rearing, or even work (if the work is elsewhere), for example a neighbourhood of old people's flats close to public housing with a reputation for crime. In the ghetto, the effects of segregation and social solidarity are in opposition but often strong. Community support in a ghetto may not be extreme but it may be very unstable as small changes in the countervailing influences may produce large changes in the mediation of fears.

The most dramatic effect of outsider theory is the stigmatised neighbourhood. If *everybody* believes crime is committed by someone else somewhere else, who then is the culprit? The common answer is minority groups which lack the power to refute the claims, whether true or not, of the majority. So gypsies, Irish, coloured immigrants in Britain, blacks, American Indians, Puerto Ricans, Mexican Americans in the United States – the list is very long – are blamed for crime (and other things besides). If the minority has spatial identity the process is strengthened. Indeed so strong is the projection of criminality onto others, that it can take place in the absence of obvious ethnic or cultural traits in the recipient group. Damer (1974) gives a graphic account of how a small urban renewal community in Glasgow achieved a reputation for criminality and other forms of deviance. Initially false, the reputation gradually became true as the members of the community lived up to the expectations imposed on them from the outside. So the stigma becomes the reality.

Damer's careful analysis highlights a major difficulty with the notion of a supportive community. It is very rare to find consistent causes and effects among the relationships we have been discussing. Does fear reduce solidarity or is greater fear caused by lack of solidarity? Is the threat of crime heightened by weak support from the community or does lack of support exaggerate the need to externalise fears? There is a pressing need to elaborate these links in a wide range of social environments.

(c) The Responsive Community

The ideas of normative and supportive communities deal with the relationships between and among individuals and groups. These relationships, however, possess an important quality: they are dynamic. Change is endemic if only at a basal level of birth and death. Individuals age and change their responsibilities at different stages in the life cycle. Community change reflects not only the changes among its members but also changes in membership. If changes in membership are great and the newcomers and leavers differ in age, social status, etc., then community change can be dramatically quick in comparison to individual change. The responsiveness of the community to changes in individual perceptions and fears of crime mediates the need to externalise threats. A responsive community provides means of representation through formal political channels or informal presssure groups. More important, perhaps, it provides channels of communication so that the meaning of the threat can be disseminated. For crime, this implies channels of communication with the agents of control – police, courts, etc. The unresponsive community promotes isolation and feelings of alienation and creates exaggerated personal responses to threats – extreme withdrawal or extreme action in the form of vigilantism or rioting.

Community responses are exaggerated by individual ambivalence to change. Stability is dull but safe, change is exciting but risky. Change is a switch from regular to new: if enough personal thresholds are reached simultaneously the community change appears very rapid. The responsive community, therefore, needs not only to provide the channels but to allow them to operate swiftly.

(d) The Legitimating Community

In areas where the crime rate is high and fears are great a collective response to crime may develop. There is evidence that the collective response may transcend individual responses in form and strength (Conklin, 1975). If the elements of a supportive and responsive community are weakly developed then the collective response may be dominant. In other words, if the normal coping mechanisms for externalising fears of victimisation and its consequences are inadequate, special mechanisms may develop. A good example is the rash of Urban Civilian Police Patrol groups which sprang up in the United States in the late 1960s (Marx and Archer, 1971, 1973). Such responses are rare and often transient, meeting particular needs at a particular time. Yet the primary element in collective reactions to crime – the legitimation of response by the community – may be important in other ways. It may underpin, for example, threshold levels of reporting or of individual commitments to react to crime as a witness. This particular form of legitimation is likely to be more significant when norms are weak or conflicting.

The term 'defended neighbourhood' has been coined to describe communities in which social control is prescribed by informal channels (Suttles, 1972). Responses to crime are but one element in the social fabric of such areas which is characterised by fear, suspicion and distrust. Confidence in the police is low and relations with them may be antagonistic. Spatial identity reinforces the legitimating power of the community by clarifying definitions of 'them' and 'us'. Juvenile gangs use similar territorial markers.

It will be clear that these four models of the community as a base of social reactions to crime are neither discrete nor comprehensive. Each places a different emphasis on the way in which individuals are located in the social environment. All, however, point to the importance of such location in understanding perceptions, fears and attitudes in relation to crime. The neighbourhood is more than a mere frame for social reactions to crime; it is an independent element in their formation.

5 THE DISTRIBUTION OF JUSTICE

Such are the conflicts and contradictions within the aims of even a single justice system that it is not surprising to find considerable disparities in outcome. Protection, deterrence, retribution and correction are perhaps the major purposes of a penal code but sentences can also serve more particular needs – to make an example; to denounce a specific form of criminal act; or to be humane. The sanctions employed by the law have become increasingly complex. Incarceration is generally viewed as a deterrent but also protects through incapacitation. Particularly with institutions for juveniles it may also be held to have corrective value. Rehabilitation, once the preserve of probation, now covers a wide range of measures, such as community service orders, week-end custody, custody and control orders, etc. as legislators and courts have struggled to make justice fair yet effective.

The driving force behind the growing range of sanctions has been a concern for the 'individualisation' of justice (Bottomley, 1973). Greater attempts have been made to fit the punishment not just to the harm suffered but to the needs of the individual offender. This has led to a harsher light being shed on the contradictions and at the same time to the devolution of greater discretion to the servants of the penal system. Disparities have always existed: whether they have become greater is questionable but they have certainly become more subject to publicity and public scrutiny.

Three major problems confront us in this chapter when examining the distribution of justice in different places:

(a) Differences in Criminal Justice Systems

There are very few acts which receive universal sanction under the law. Different countries, different societies have evolved different systems of coping with behaviour regarded as antisocial. Criminal codes vary widely in the definition of sanctionable acts and in the sanctions employed. Moreover, the relations between the various arms of the justice system – police, legal profession, judiciary and prison service, etc. – are far from uniform. An attempt to associate differences in the content and structure of criminal justice systems with differences in their economic, social and cultural background may well be a fruitful exercise (cf. David and Scott's (1973) comparison of Toledo, Ohio and

Rosario, Argentina) but such cross-national comparisons are beyond the scope of this book. On a particular issue, different policymaking strategies or legislative philosophies may produce different consequences in terms of crime – for example the introduction of car steering-locks in Britain and Germany had rather different effects on their respective rates of car theft (Mayhew *et al.*, 1980). Even within a single country, federal systems can play havoc with equality of justice. Harries and Brunn (1978) have outlined some of the variations in statutes which exist among US states, which they suggest are closely related to differences in regional social philosophy.

While we cannot deal with environmental factors at the inter-system end of the scale, recognition of differences between systems in response to essentially the same problem can often highlight particular relations within a single system and lead us to be a little more cautious in locating the source of disparities, even in assigning meaning to what we consider disparity. For example, compared to the Netherlands, imprisonment rates in Britain are roughly four times as high, in New Zealand five times and in the United States fifteen times. Yet the proportionate rise in crime in all four countries over the last three decades has been substantially the same.

(b) Problems of Defining the Legitimacy of Disparities in Justice

Disparities in justice emerge from the differentiation of offences and offenders while being processed by the criminal justice system. Differentiation is primarily a consequence of the discretion which is available to and used by the servants of the system. The crucial, but problematic, question is the extent to which discretion is exercised in favour of *legally-relevant* or *-irrelevant* factors. At one pole is the discretion laid down by the law: courts must take into account the nature and seriousness of the offence and the law normally stipulates a range of penalties for a given category. Likewise, the courts will differentiate offenders in relation to their previous criminal record and the number of charges brought forward. More informal, less tangible but still legally-relevant are factors which relate to the status of the offender (age, family responsibilities, employment situation, etc.) and to the circumstances of the offence (for example whether there was premeditation or provocation). The attitude of the offender (voluntary admissions or statements of contrition) may also be important.

On the other side of the coin, legally-irrelevant factors which may be significant include the sex, race or socio-economic status of offenders, presence or absence of legal representation, plea-bargaining, the quality of information available to the decision-maker. Even the demeanour or appearance of offenders may have an effect.

The problem is not so much that discretion exists and that it can do much to explain disparities in justice but rather that it is difficult to draw a line between the relevant and irrelevant categories. Nobody denies that murder should attract a more severe penalty than pick-pocketing, nor that the personal prejudices of judges should be extraneous to their decisions. Yet between the extremes is a smooth transition with few clearly demarcated boundaries. The factor of age illustrates the difficulties. I have placed it in the relevant category, yet Hagan (1974) regards it as legally irrelevant. At different levels both categorisations are appropriate. Broad distinctions of age are relevant – adult versus juvenile – but fine distinctions not. Hagan reviews twenty studies of sentencing and concludes that in general extra-legal factors have little effect, though there are some specific exceptions. My own case study of Hull (reported below) will reach broadly similar conclusions from a rather narrower perspective.

The degree to which geographical disparities in justice reflect differences in the distribution of legal criteria has received scant attention in the literature. We must, therefore, avoid rushing to conclude that observed disparities reflect unwarranted bias in distribution of justice.

(c) Problem of Deciding Who Dispenses Justice

To this point we have been treating justice as the responsibility of the courts. Yet we know that only a proportion of offenders reach this stage. Both victims and the agents of the criminal justice system (notably the police, but also probation officers and court officials) exercise discretion through their decisions about who or who not to report, charge, caution, indict, etc. In terms of numbers such pre-trial decisions far exceed the more formal dispositions of the courts, though the more serious the offence, the further it is likely to proceed along the path to court.

There have been few attempts to extricate disparities consistently thoughout the various stages in the process of a case from incident to court. None have considered disparities between areas in other than an *ad hoc* manner. The task is in any case complicated by lack of consistency among the routes to court, for example between adult and juvenile offenders or between different types of offences. Evidence of the exercise of discretion and its effects is well reviewed by Bottomley (1973). An illustration of the extent of pre-trial decision-making is provided by Thornberry's (1973) study of juvenile justice in Philadelphia. Of the 9,601 cases of officially recorded delinquency in which the final disposition was known, 67.9 per cent were handled entirely by the police. Of the remainder who were referred to the juvenile court, some 43.4 per cent were dismissed or discharged at a preliminary hearing. Of those referred for formal appearance at the juvenile court, 37.4 per cent received an institutional sentence (just 6.8 per cent of the original total). Thornberry also examines the effect of the legally irrelevant factors of race and socio-economic status while attempting to control for the legally relevant factors of the seriousness of the offence and recidivism. At all three levels he finds that race and socio-economic status have effects on decisions independent of the legally relevant factors, although the effects were rather less at preliminary hearing than at the police stage or formal court appearance. The consequence of these biases is a progressive increase in the proportion of blacks and low socio-economic status offenders as justice proceeds: 49 per cent of decisions by the police to handle the matter themselves involved blacks compared to 82 per cent of institutional sentences. Thornberry's conclusions contradict the more general comments of Hagan (1974) referred to above (Thornberry's study was not one of those reviewed by Hagan). However, Thornberry's data are for juveniles only and this specification may be critical as we shall see in the case study below. What is clear is that disparities exist in justice outside the province of the courts. These may differ in nature and extent but will, through the selection process, have an impact on the composition of the offender-stock who reach the courts. Magistrates and judges may be consistent in their application of discretion towards legitimate goals yet this very consistency may merely reproduce disparities already built-in at an earlier stage of the criminal justice process.

Disparities in the Distribution of Justice

(a) Regional Variations

Harries and Lura (1974) have observed patterns of sentencing in the United States. Using the 89 judicial districts they show that 1970 Average Sentence Weights (a composite index using a weighting system to equate different sentences) varied from 2.6 in Louisiana West to 12.7 in Alabama South. Little regional trend is apparent, with severity of sentence a patchwork of highs and lows throughout the country. Even using Relative Sentence Weights (the difference between actual weighted sentences and the weighted sentences expected if national average sentences were applied to each district's set of offences) does not greatly clarify the pattern. The patterns for probation – the largest category – are also examined in both percentage and relative forms and yield a more explicit trend. Use of probation tends to be high in the northwest and low in the southwest and southeast. The authors attempt a three-region generalisation of all four patterns. Districts most favourable to defendents are mostly located in the northern half of the country; districts least favourable cluster in the lower Mississippi Valley and along the Gulf coast. Although statistically significant, this regionalisation is not regarded as rigorous by the authors. More penetrating is their analysis of possible explanatory factors behind the rather diffuse patterns. Among the legally relevant factors, only percentage of defendants with a prior prison record made a consistent contribution to the predictability of sentencing variation. The distribution of offence types was not important and the use of observation reports was significant only for average sentence weights (the authors do not comment on whether the effect was favourable or unfavourable). Legally irrelevant variables were, if anything, slightly more important as predictors of sentencing patterns but none consistently. Variations in court procedure produced some relationships; variables related to the characteristics of the districts' judges did not. This analysis, while perhaps flawed by its level of generalisation, is important for the degree of disparity in sentencing that exists even at this highly aggregated level.

Regional variations in England and Wales of the use of probation are also evident (Barr and O'Leary, 1966). The percentage (for 1961) varies from 26.2 per cent in the south, through 22.7 per cent in the Midlands, 20.3 per cent in Wales, 18.2 per cent in the north, down to 16.9 per cent in London. Disregarding the anomaly of London, the regional trend is therefore the reverse of the United States where the north was more favoured by the use of probation. Probation in England and Wales is inversely related to the official crime rate. Regions with more use of probation have also more use of social enquiry reports and use longer probation orders. Unrelated to use of probation were caseloads, proportion of trained staff or degree of successful completion of the orders. Although this study is again highly generalised it seems to indicate some regional consistency in the sentencing behaviour – consistencies perhaps in the relationships between courts and the areas they serve.

The granting of legal aid in Britain is another area where considerable discretion exists, and where there are wide discrepancies both at regional and local scale (Levenson, 1980a). Normally, legal aid will be granted under a means test and if the interests of justice are served

(Legal Aid Act 1974). For adults on trial for indictable offences in England and Wales, the proportion of legal-aid defendants has been rising and in 1979 stood at 60 per cent The proportion of legal aid applications refused by magistrates varies considerably between police force areas from a high of 33.7 per cent in Gwent to a low of 5.8 per cent in Cambridgeshire (1979 rates). Within police force areas disparities are just as large (Home Office, 1980, Table 25). In London, the consistently high proportion of refusals at one particular court has attracted a degree of public attention (Kettle, 1979); otherwise the disparities are of the same order as elsewhere (Levenson, 1980a, 1980b). Regrettably these studies while ventilating the extent of inequality, offer little by way of explanation of the patterns.

(b) Urban-rural Differences

Contrasts between urban and rural situations receive a more penetrating treatment in Hagan's (1977) study of the Province of Alberta, Canada. In the specific context of the treatment of minority group offenders (Indians and part-Indians), he contrasts the role played by various factors, legal and extra-legal, in the judicial process in urban and rural areas. Pre-sentence recommendations of probation officers in urban areas tend to reflect legally relevant criteria and to show greater uniformity. Rural probation officers' recommendations exhibit greater straightforward prejudice and are more likely to be mediated by the officer's evaluation of the success prospects of treatment. These contrasts, Hagan suggests, relate not just to urbanisation but also to the bureaucratisation of the judicial process. The urban situation yields a different social setting from which offences emerge, for example restrictions on personal space and privacy, or greater demands for conformity with material standards. Urban courts, therefore, have to deal with group differences which are endemic and which no equality of treatment can eradicate. Rural courts are less overloaded, less professional and less hierarchical: and Indians are recommended more severe sentences without recourse to legally relevant justifications. Moreover, Indians in rural communities are more likely to be sent to prison in default of fine payments than their urban counterparts. There are parallels here with the more severe sentencing of blacks by rural courts in California (Pope, 1975).

The main lesson of Hagan's work is that, irrespective of whatever disparities exist, decision-making in urban and rural communities takes place in very different judicial environments. In another Canadian study, Hogarth (1971) points out some of the disparities and discusses the differences in judicial attitudes which underpin them. Urban magistrates in Ontario are less likely to give suspended sentences (with or without probation), short-term prison sentences or reformatory sentences. They are more likely to fine or to use longer terms of ordinary imprisonment, or to give penitentiary sentences. Some of the differences may be accounted for by the types of case appearing before the magistrates but there are other differences. Urban magistrates tend on the whole to be rather more punitive and to place more emphasis on notions of justice and social defence. Rural magistrates score more highly on beliefs in the reformation of offenders but less on the general deterrence of punishment. There was, however, considerable variation within both urban and rural groups with some overlap between them. The urban group of magistrates exhibited heterogeneity in a number of areas – a reflection, Hogarth suggests, of greater proximity and interaction working towards a polarisation of beliefs and attitudes. Rural magistrates are more isolated, rely more on contacts with the community than among themselves, and are less likely to have a poor image of this community. Their decisions owe less to the application of any particular rationale of justice than to the perceived needs of the specific community.

(c) Local Variations

Disparities in justice at the local level are no less wide. Imprisonment rates (for adult indictable property offenders) in Britain ranged from 3 per cent to 55 per cent in 1951-4 (Hood, 1962) and there appeared to be no consistent relationship between the rate and the characteristics of the men before the court. At about the same period, but for a rather different set of offences, Lunden (1957) found a range of imprisonment rates from 10.2 per cent to 37.8 per cent among the judicial districts of Iowa. A decade later, Patchett and McClean (1965) examined the activities of a number of juvenile courts in northern England and found marked differences between ostensibly similar places. In Ontario, Canada imprisonment rates for common gaols (usually short sentences) ranged from 4 per cent to 60 per cent among judicial districts in 1964 (Hogarth, 1971).

For particular offence categories differences also exist. Harries and Brunn (1978) trace trends in sentencing for drug offences in Oklahoma with some surprising results contradictory to their expectations. In a more synoptic review of the sentencing of cannabis offenders in Britain, Ealand (1976) reveals an apparent lack of trend in either the severity or the consistency among courts. One place not to get caught, though, is Guernsey where your holiday is almost certain to be extended at Her Majesty's pleasure. For motoring offences, the sentencing practices of individual magistrates tend to be consistent, that among magistrates serving the same court considerably less so, and the residual disparities between courts very wide (Hood, 1972).

Place-to-place variations in justice are indeed a Pandora's box with many discrepancies there to attract the unwary. Generalisations neither superficial nor tied up with specifics are less easy to come by and need a careful evaluation of a complex range of factors.

Residential Bias in Court Sentencing: A Case Study

The scope of this case study is deliberately narrow in order to limit the role of extraneous factors. It considers only the decisions reached by the courts in a single, medium-sized British city. Its aim is to assess the extent to which there are differences in sentencing patterns between different residential environments. The crucial issue to be examined is not the extent and nature of the disparities themselves but rather the ways in which their extent and nature may be mediated by a relationship between a court's decision and the community it serves. Observing differences between magistrates courts, Hood (1962) showed that imprisonment policies vary considerably and he implicated the social characteristics of the area served, the social constitution of the bench and its particular view of the crime problem. If the attitudes and perception of magistrates and judges are as important as we implied when looking at some of the general patterns of disparity, then it is reasonable to hypothesise that such extra-legal discretion could apply not just between communities as Hood suggests but between the constituent parts of a court's area of jurisdiction. Do, for instance, magistrates have a common perception of the 'criminal areas' of the community and, if so, is this being used in association with beliefs about the effectiveness of various types of sentence in different social milieus? The home address of offenders is one of the few consistent pieces of information available to the court and may be used in conjunction with the age and appearance to fix a 'social location' for the defendant that may have a significant effect on his treatment.

(a) The Data

The data are derived from a 14 per cent sample of crime reports for the City of Hull in 1972. Supplementary information was obtained from

CID files on known offenders. The reference set for the analysis comprises all charges, police cautions and offences taken-into-consideration (TIC) which resulted from the sample of incidents notified to the police. It is not a set of court cases, since a single case may involve a number of offenders and an even larger number of incidents. Nor is it a set of offenders since this would mean ignoring a fair proportion of the decisions handed down. The choice of this particular reference set was influenced by the need to approach as near as possible the sum of the activity of the courts. It does mean that some offences are included in the total more than once – if more than one offender was involved – and some offenders are also double counted if they committed more than one offence. The total sample for the reference set is 1,317, though there are minor absences of data on some of the test criteria.

The residential environment of offenders is based on a fourfold classification of social areas in the city. Areas were classified on the results of a factor analysis of 1971 Census data (Davidson and Francis, 1973). The four types of residential backgrounds may be loosely labelled according to their position on the two main dimensions of social differentiation in the city – socio-economic status and housing tenure/amenities. *Owner-occupied* areas are generally high status, and have a good standard of housing amenities. *Mixed* areas are medium in status and tend to have a variety of owning and renting. *Inner-city* areas are low in status and score worst on housing standards. *Council* areas are characterised by low status but a good standard of housing amenities. Due to the poor fit of census boundaries to social divides in some areas and the close mixture of very different residential types in other areas, these labels must necessarily be loose. Selection of 'pure' residential types – if this is possible – would very likely result in clearer patterns of differentiation, but also ignore the heterogeneity which is characteristic of many parts of the city.

(b) Analysis

The distribution of sentences within the four types of residential area is shown in Table 5.1. The majority of offenders whose charges result in a prison sentence are resident in inner-city areas, although such residents are involved in only a third of all dispositions. Such a preponderance may reflect a concentration of more serious offenders in these areas. The pattern is not, however, repeated for other custodial sentences (mostly to other institutions for juveniles). Proportionally, residents of owner-occupied areas are most likely to be sentenced thus. Neither suspended prison sentences nor probation and other super-

Table 5.1: Sentencing and Offenders' Residential Environment: Hull, 1972

	All areas		Offender's residential area type							
Sentence[a]			Owner-occupied		Mixed		Council housing		Inner-city	
	No.	%	No.	%	No.	%	No.	%	No.	%
Prison	95	7	4	2	12	8	28	5	51	11
Other institution	144	11	31	19	9	6	56	10	48	11
Suspended sentence	69	5	7	4	5	3	23	4	34	7
Probation/ supervision	221	17	23	14	22	15	89	16	87	19
Fine	398	30	43	27	50	33	189	34	116	26
Conditional discharge	119	9	18	11	19	13	50	9	32	7
Police caution	123	9	13	8	15	10	56	10	39	9
Absolute discharge, other	66	5	6	4	7	5	33	6	20	4
Not guilty	15	1	5	3	2	1	4	1	4	1
Not known	67	5	12	7	9	6	23	4	23	5
Total[b]	1317	100	162	100	150	100	551	100	454	100

a. Sentences refer to charges, offences taken-into-consideration (TIC) and police cautions (see definition in text).

b. Percentage columns may not add up due to rounding.

Source: Davidson (1977), Table 1.

vision orders show much differentiation between areas, though the latter is slightly more common among inner-city residents. Fines are less common at both ends of the social scale, reflecting perhaps the diminished effectiveness of monetary retribution among the better-off or inability to pay among the poor. Conditional discharge is more common among residents of higher status areas both owner-occupied and mixed. Cautions and absolute discharges are very weakly differentiated. Being found not guilty is extremely rare in Hull, but too much should not be read into this as Hull has less serious crime and there tends to be an inverse relationship between seriousness of offence and chances of being found guilty.

These differences are interesting but could be extremely misleading. In the first place they may simply reflect the fact that the circumstances in which statutory and other legally-relevant forms of discretion should be applied are not themselves evenly distributed within the city. Inner-city residents may be more likely to commit serious crimes, have a criminal record or commit more offences. Council estates may have more residents in the high-risk juvenile age-groups, etc. In order to test whether the disparities in sentencing reflect purely residential bias a series of chi-square tests was run involving eleven criteria spanning the range of possible sources of discretion. For each criterion the pattern of sentences was evaluated for the four residential area types. If the distribution of sentences was consistent among the areas, residential bias cannot be imputed, irrespective of the overall pattern. To preserve reasonable cell frequencies for this exercise sentences were grouped into: custody (prison or other institution), supervision (including suspended sentence and probation), fine, and discharge (conditional or absolute plus caution). The few not guilty decisions are included with the discharges and decision not known cases were excluded. The results of this exercise are summarised in Table 5.2 (for further details see Davidson, 1977). The eleven criteria fall naturally in five groups:

(i) Seriousness of the Offence. This is obviously the most important source of variation in sentencing. It is, however, the most difficult to measure across the whole range of criminal offences (cf. Sellin and Wolfgang, 1964). The test criterion selected – *value of goods stolen* – only applies to thefts, though these comprised 67 per cent of detected offences. The overall disparities are considerable but hardly surprising: smaller thefts attract 'lighter' sentences. However, the pattern is not consistent for residents of all areas. For minor thefts inner-city residents are more likely to get custody or supervision, and offenders from owner-occupied areas to be discharged but not to be fined. For larger thefts, residents of owner-occupied areas are more likely to be fined and not given custodial sentences. None of these differences are particularly strong.

In order to test the effect of seriousness a further, rather different strategy may be adopted – to select a particular offence and repeat the analysis. Shoplifting was chosen since it encompasses a rather narrow range of seriousness and it was, moreover, the largest single category. Of the eleven criteria, four were not applicable to shoplifting (e.g. no victim knew the offender) and five had similar patterns of residential bias to that for all crimes. In only two cases were disparities different from the general pattern and then not always markedly. So the weak

Table 5.2: Sentencing Disparities and Residential Environment: Hull, 1972

Test criterion	Extent of disparities in sentencing on test criterion	Differences between residential environments in pattern of sentencing disparities on test criterion
Seriousness of crime		
(1) value stolen	very strong	slight
Status of offender before court		
(2) Sex	very strong	considerable
(3) Age	very strong	considerable
(4) Previous criminal record	very strong	none
(5) Known to have committed other offences in current year	very strong	none
Offender's background		
(6) Occupation	very strong	none
(7) Employment status	very strong	none
Circumstances of offence		
(8) Group/single offender	weak	considerable
(9) Type of area where offence committed	very strong	slight
(1) Victim knew/did not know offender prior to offence	weak	slight
Process of case		
(11) Dealt with by Magistrates/Crown Court	very strong	considerable

Source: Davidson (1977), Table 2.

inconsistencies related to the value of goods stolen are not disturbed. The rather tentative conclusion must be that variations in the seriousness of offending are partly but not completely responsible for sentencing differences.

(ii) The Status of the Offender Before the Court. Disparities in sentencing related to *sex* are very strong. The tendency of males to be more likely to receive custodial sentences is replicated in all types of residential areas, as is the roughly equal proportion of males and females fined. However, there is a strong tendency for females from both inner-city areas and council estates to be discharged, whereas supervision is more prevalent in high status areas.

Of all the criteria tested it is perhaps *age* which produces the greatest inconsistencies among areas and these relate primarily to young offenders. In all areas adults (aged 21+ years) are more likely to be fined and less likely to be discharged. Juveniles (aged 10-16) are, for obvious reasons, unlikely to be fined irrespective of their residential background. The inconsistencies are most clearly highlighted by the contrast between owner-occupied and inner-city areas. Juveniles from owner-occupied areas are very markedly more likely to receive custodial sentences (i.e. detention centre, community home, etc.) than offenders of the same age group in the inner-city – 34 per cent compared to 16 per cent. Since the number of charges, etc., emanating from residents at these social extremes is approximately equal, the curious fact emerges that the majority of court decisions resulting in custody for juveniles involves offenders from high status areas. For youths (aged 17-20), this polarity is reversed: 12 per cent of offenders in this age group from high status areas end up in custody, compared to 37 per cent of offenders from the inner-city.

The other two criteria in this group refer to *recidivism* and *multiple offending* (whether known to have committed other offences in the current year). While the overall pattern exhibits a high degree of differentiation of offenders on these counts, in neither case are there significant inconsistencies between areas. This seems a little surprising in view of the disparities over age. It tends to suggest, moreover, that the age disparities are not reflections of variations in recidivism or multiple offending between areas. This is illustrated in Tables 5.3 and 5.4. Both consider males only, since the patterns are slightly stronger for males, and both ignore police cautioning. In Table 5.3 we can see that a higher proportion of boys from owner-occupied areas have a previous criminal record but boys from this type of area and the inner-city are

Table 5.3: Sentence, Residential Environment and Recidivism, Boys Aged 10-16: Hull, 1972

Charges and TICs of boys aged 10-16		Offender's residential area type			
		Owner-occupied	Mixed	Council housing	Inner-city
Boys with no previous criminal record	Number[a]	27	16	97	45
	% resulting in custody	30	19	13	13
Boys with previous criminal record	Number[a]	26	7	71	16
	% resulting in custody	77	14	21	31

a. Number of charges and TICs, Magistrates Court.
Source: Davidson (1977), Table 3.

Table 5.4: Sentence, Residential Environment and Recidivism, Youths Aged 17-20: Hull, 1972

Charges and TICs of youths aged 17-20		Offender's residential area type			
		Owner-occupied	Mixed	Council housing	Inner-city
Youths with no previous criminal record	Number[a]	6	7	22	16
	% resulting in custody	0	0	5	38
Youths with previous criminal record	Number[a]	4	15	59	68
	% resulting in custody	50	33	32	44

a. Number of charges and TICs, Magistrates and Crown Courts.
Source: Davidson (1977), Table 4.

both 2½ times more likely to be placed in custody if they have a criminal record. The disparity between these types of area we noted earlier for this age group therefore applies to both first offenders and to recidivists. Among youths, on the other hand, the proportion of recidivists placed in custody does not vary so greatly from area to area, but inner-city areas are exceptional for the high proportion of first offenders that get custody. At 38 per cent it is nearly as high as the 44 per cent of recidivsts.

(iii) Offender's Background. Although sentences are strongly differentiated on both offender's *occupation* and *employment status*, the patterns are consistent for all residential areas. Since the residential typology relies very heavily on these sorts of criteria at the ecological level, the absence of bias here does tend to suggest that where it occurs elsewhere it is not only derived from individual circumstances. It is not just middle-class or working-class people who are favoured or otherwise (although this may be true) but people from a particular residential environment irrespective of their personal situation.

(iv) Circumstances of the Offence. There is a slight tendency for *joint offenders* (where more than one was involved in a particular offence) to be punished more harshly than the lone offender. This pattern is, however, not consistent across the residential types. The greatest contrast is between owner-occupied areas and council estates. Both have similar slight majorities of joint offenders, but the courts are more punitive to joint offenders resident in owner-occupied areas and do not differentiate among residents of council estates on this factor.

The *locus of the offence* produces strong differentiation among sentences which is not consistently replicated in all areas. Offences committed in the city centre tend to attract fines and not custodial sentences and this is true wherever the offender lives. Offences committed elsewhere than the city centre tend to be in the offender's own type of residential area, but there is little support for the view that 'fouling one's own backyard' is a consistent source of disparity. Residents of owner-occupied and council areas are more likely to receive custodial sentences for offending in their own type of area, but offenders from mixed and inner-city areas are not.

The *anonymity of the offender* varies little from area to area. About a quarter of victims know their attacker and in general the courts tend to be more lenient if this is so. However, this distinction arises mainly from a significantly more punitive attitude towards the anonymous offender from owner-occupied areas. In neither of the two low status areas do the courts appear to differentiate on this criterion.

(v) Process of Case. The final criterion examines the influence of the *type of court* responsible for the sentence. Magistrates, being by definition members of the community, might be expected to have more accurate knowledge or perceptions of its residential environments than circuit judges. Since the Crown Courts in general take only the more serious cases, there are, not unexpectedly, marked differences in the proportion of sentences handed down: 65 per cent of Crown Court decisions result in custody, whereas 63 per cent of magisterial sentences involve a fine or one of the forms of discharge. However, this general pattern is only replicated for offenders from lower status areas (both inner-city and council estates). By contrast, there is no significant difference between the courts in sentences handed down to residents of owner-occupied areas. The variation arises primarily as a result of the fact that magistrates are responsible for 83 per cent of custodial sentences to offenders from owner-occupied areas, compared to 47 per cent for the city as a whole. This is indeed a striking disparity between the courts. It mostly involves juveniles and may have changed as the Criminal Justice Act (1972) has moved some of magistrates' sentencing powers to the Crown Court.

(c) Discussion

From the pattern of court decisions, it seems clear that while there is evidence of some spatial bias in the distribution of justice, it is neither general nor consistent in favouring offenders from particular residential backgrounds at the expense of others. There is some support for the view that class bias exists – non-manual offenders tend to be fined, manual workers are more likely to get custodial sentences – but it arises not so much from perceptions of social milieu as from information before the court about individuals. Differentiation similarly exists on the basis of the seriousness of the offence and of the criminal record of the offender. On these criteria the power of the courts to discriminate is seen to apply but without spatial bias except in a few minor instances. It is what you are and what you have done, not where you live, that appear to count.

There are, however, two main areas where disparities between residential environments do occur. Perhaps the more significant of these concerns the sex and age of offenders, particularly male juveniles. The distribution of sentences in inner-city areas seems to imply a connection between the role of the court and residential background. Supervisory sentences are most common among very young offenders (53 per cent of first offenders under 17 get probation or supervision orders) but for older boys sentences are much more severe. This would fit well with paternalistic assumptions among sentencers about the need for 'care and protection' of inner-city boys from the criminogenic influences of their social milieu. Older youths, on the other hand, are the main purveyors of such influences, and as such need excision like rotten apples. If the courts do discriminate in this way, they need both an awareness of which are the 'high risk' areas and an attitude towards the role of sentencing in society. That the attitudes exist and are important has been shown by a number of studies (Green, 1961; Wheeler *et al.*, 1968; Hogarth, 1971; Hood, 1972). Hogarth in particular concludes that judicial attitudes with respect to the aims of the penal system and its various sanctions are one of the major sources of disparities in sentencing. Hood furthermore suggests that the attitudes of the bench are more important than those of individual magistrates. Magistrates' perceptions of the location and character of criminal areas have not been investigated, but would be unlikely to be less strong than those we have discussed more generally in Chapter 4. A common perception of the criminality of various residential environments in the city allied with particular attitudes towards the role of sentencing seems the most likely explanation for the pattern of court decisions on young offenders from inner-city areas in Hull. Nevertheless, another bench in another city may have different attitudes and different perceptions (Hood, 1972).

The treatment of juveniles from owner-occupied areas is very different and not easy to equate with the inner-city situation. The main difficulty is the greater use of custodial sentences, especially by magistrates. These, however, are predominantly not prison, but other institutions such as detention centres and community homes, and relate to *younger* boys from owner-occupied areas: older youths are more likely to be the subject of probation or supervision orders. The attitude which underpins this pattern may be corrective rather than punitive. Boys from middle-class backgrounds may be seen to have had the advantage of a supportive environment (unlike inner-city boys). The fact that they have offended may engender a more positive response among magistrates who share a similar background – a need to correct (the individual's wrong) rather than protect (from other individuals' wrongs) as in the case of boys from a perceived poor environment. Wheeler *et al.* (1968) note an apparently paradoxical relationship among Boston judges between 'punitive' sentencing and 'enlightened' attitudes: they suggest that it arises from a belief among 'progressive' judges that institutions can provide a better corrective or supportive environment. The need to protect the community may be more keenly felt than in inner-city areas leading to earlier excision. The fact that, as we have already noted, recidivists are not treated relatively more harshly implies corrective rather than punitive motives. If this interpretation is valid then the parameters of the offender-sentence-community model vary with the perceived character of the community. With middle-class communities, the dominant themes are correction for the individual and protection for the community. With inner-city areas, the concern focuses on a more passive protection of the individual.

The other area where spatial inconsistencies exist is related to the circumstances of the offence. Here the disparities are weaker and the pattern seems altogether more complex. Both joint and anonymous offenders tend to receive custodial sentences – a pattern that is clearest among offenders from owner-occupied areas. By contrast, offenders from council estates are not differentiated on either count, but are more likely to be placed in custody if they offend in their own type of area. An implication of this may be a recognition by the courts of the problems of estate living, again especially for younger offenders. Circumstances that elsewhere might lead to more severe sentences may be discounted on estates, for example gang or group activities. Armstrong and Wilson (1973) give a graphic account of these problems but do not examine patterns of sentencing in detail. The effect of situational factors on subsequent treatment is a little-researched aspect of crime and it is difficult to be more than tentative that perceptions and attitudes are again shaping decisions.

Bearing in mind the rather generalised nature of the data used for this case study, it nevertheless seems reasonable to conclude that the courts at root appear to be expressing some fairly well-formed, if specific, attitudes towards the perceived residential environment of offenders. Bottomley (1973) suggests that there is support for two rather different interpretations of the relationship between courts and communities. Magistrates either retain their pre-existing attitudes and do not make specific reference to the community in decision-making or they act directly on behalf of perceived interests in the community. The evidence reviewed here tends to favour the latter view in a quite positive way. The role of the sentence as a mediation between offender and society is being given a different interpretation in different social milieus: what goes for the boy from a slum environment may not go for the boy from a well-to-do suburb, nor indeed the boy living on a large council estate. However, as Bottomley points out, this raises questions about the validity of taking into account community norms and values, not to speak of those of the decision-makers. It also raises questions about the accuracy of the perceptions of residential background upon which decisions are made.

Justice and the Community

The evidence implicating community factors in decision-making within the criminal justice system is patchy and diffuse. Justice itself is seen to serve many masters and among these the community is not often prominent. Yet crime is only crime because of the social reaction to it, however attenuated this link has become. Sometimes the public outcry at, for example, a wave of muggings or a series of gruesome murders may provoke a direct judicial response aimed at and for the community (see for example Hall *et al.*, 1978). Exemplary sentences frequently have such a motive. At a more basal level, all decision-makers, judiciary, police or whatever, operate within an environment which legitimates their powers of discretion, both formally and informally. Many decision-makers have, moreover, strong roots in the community which they serve (Hood, 1962; Hogarth, 1971).

John Hogarth in his thorough analysis of sentencing behaviour among Ontario magistrates provides some substance to the relations between judicial attitudes and penal philosophies and the character of the communities serviced (Hogarth, 1971). Five distinct sets of attitudes are identified: 'justice' is offence orientated and reflects concerns that the punishment is fair and appropriate in relation to the seriousness of the crime; 'punishment corrects' is offender orientated and reflects beliefs in the efficacy of individual deterrence through punishment and confidence in the penal institutions which carry it out; 'intolerance' locates crime within a wider perspective of social deviance; 'social defence' encompasses notions of crime as a threat to the social order and that punishment should be aimed at deterring potential offenders; and finally 'modernism' incorporates the kinds of values which underpin the modern welfare state and opposes the traditional values of the puritan ethic (crime as sin, etc.). These attitudes are related to the use of certain types of sentence. For example, magistrates who make frequent use of suspended sentence without probation tend to have less concern for justice, to believe that punishment does not correct, and to be more tolerant and modernist. Particularly for less serious cases this sort of liberal, non-punitive sentencing philosophy is likely to be associated with less use of imprisonment compared to magistrates who are more traditional in outlook and intolerant in their attitudes.

The relationship between attitudes and the characteristics of the communities served is strong. Magistrates with high justice scores tend to serve in large cities with mixed ethnic populations and many recent immigrants from Continental Europe. Punishment corrects is more typical of magistrates from newer, expanding communities on the periphery of the large cities where incomes are higher than average and the crime rate lower. Magistrates with high tolerance scores tend to serve stable, rural, French-speaking communities with a high crime rate. Emphasis on social defence is more likely among magistrates from urban areas with a high proportion of young adults. Magistrates expressing sympathy with modernist ideas tend to live in stable, British communities with neither high nor low crime rates. Hogarth concludes that magisterial attitudes are not, therefore, exempt from external influences: in many ways they reflect the problems faced by magistrates in the local community.

Beyond this direct contribution of community factors in decision-making there are other less tangible effects. We have already observed in contrasting urban and rural situations how differences in court organisation may lead to varying emphasis in the criteria selected to justify decisions (Hagan, 1974) and how the social location of the decision-maker may influence his attitudes (Hogarth, 1971). Similarly the social composition of the bench may reflect concerns within the community which are expressed through its attitudes (Hood, 1962). So it is not surprising that an urban court dealing with a high crime rate community is likely to exercise its discretion in rather different ways from a small rural court in more intimate relations to its community.

Two important questions are raised by these rather tentative reflections on the distribution of justice. The first concerns the need for a community perspective. If the trend towards the individualisation of justice is justified – that is, by regarding the fitting of punishment to the needs of the particular offender as effective in both personal and economic terms – then one element in this process should be the evaluation of the interaction between the offender and the community. If, however, emphasis is placed on the societal aims of justice, then the needs of a particular community are a distraction. We saw in Chapter 4 how important the community is as a point of reference at earlier stages in the processing of crime. To see its need now as a mere distraction is hardly appropriate.

The second question concerns the terms of reference for a community perspective. The fact that the community through the neighbourhood or ghetto effect may be exaggerated or unrealistic in its perceptions of crime does not lend confidence to accommodating its viewpoint. And yet however unrealistic perceptions may be, they are none the less real and provide a framework within which offenders as well as victims operate. The community perspective is therefore based on the social reactions to crime – perceptions of its consequences, attitudes towards the law and police, beliefs in justice, levels of tolerance of offending and more particularly offenders – and on the recognition that these are not uniform. But understanding the social reactions alone is not sufficient: what is needed also is an awareness of the relation between the offender and his social environment. If the offender's perceptions of reaction to his behaviour are at variance with the wider reaction, then setting an appropriate level of punishment is more difficult since the influence of his future social relations is that less predictable. A match between the offender's and community's expectations may facilitate decision-making but an inappropriate punishment in this case is doubly ineffective. For example, being harsh to the petty thief from a neighbourhood where pilfering is rife may alienate the thief (and perhaps as a consequence turn him into a bigger thief) on the one hand and reduce respect for the law on the other (and perhaps lead to more pilfering because less gets reported).

Differences between places in the distribution of justice are neither random nor a simple reflection of judicial bias. The major factor is variation in the differential distribution of legally relevant sources of discretion – differences in the nature and seriousness of crimes particularly. Of lesser significance but still important, are the effects of variations in attitudes and penal philosophies of decison-makers within the justice system which in turn may reflect, directly or indirectly, concerns within the communities served. Of minor importance are the effects of legally irrelevant variables, though the role of these in explaining residual inconsistencies may be significant. The extent to which the recognition of differences in community concerns is legitimate remains problematic: and takes the debate into a wider arena beyond the scope of this book – should the criteria of justice be universalistic or diffuse? Disparities in justice exist and may be explained, if partially – questions remain about the utility of these explanations.

6 THE ROLE OF ENVIRONMENTAL FACTORS IN CRIME

Interest in the environmental correlates of crime is no recent development. As we have already remarked in Chapter 3, nineteenth-century observers of poverty in London (Mayhew, 1864; Booth, 1891) noted the association between crime and slum conditions. In the early decades of this century, these links were given more formal treatment by Burt (1925) in Britain and by the Chicago school (Shaw, 1929; Shaw and McKay, 1942) and their followers. The last two decades have seen an explosion of research activity and a number of reviews have been published, notably those of Scott (1972), Harries (1974, 1980) and Herbert (1976, 1977b, 1979). The purposes of this chapter are to draw together the various ways in which environmental factors are implicated in patterns of crime and to present an overview of major arenas of interest and utility. Parts of this chapter inevitably overlap with some of the earlier comment, particularly the review of ecological theories in Chapter 3. The intention here is not to be hidebound by the constraints, for example, of aggregate or official data but to place the wide variety of relevant studies in a broad perspective of environmental roles.

Scale and Distance Effects

Proximity is a key factor in a wide range of criminal activity. Its role varies from the simple and direct effect of distance to the complex interactions and mediations implied by social mix. Across the range four arenas may be identified: in all four the emphasis here is on the role of spatial structure.

(i) Distance Decay. The simple effect of distance has been noted in a number of studies of journey-to-crime – for example Turner (1969), Stephenson (1974), Curtis (1974), Baldwin and Bottoms (1976) and Pyle (1976a, b). More sophisticated attempts at model building have been attempted by Haynes (1973) fitting distance decay functions and Lee *et al*. (1974) and Smith (1976) testing spatial interaction models. Too few of these studies pass beyond mere description but some efforts have been made to integrate distance within a conceptual frame-

work, notably by Newman (1972) in his theory of defensible space and by Carter and Hill (1976, 1979) in their analysis of criminal perceptions.

(ii) Barriers and Channels. It is evident that simple distance models do not always provide a good fit to patterns of offending. One basic reason is that perceptions of opportunity are distorted by incomplete knowledge of the environment. Spur-of-the-moment offenders, who may well be in the majority, derive their knowledge from the range presented by legitimate activities which are spatially constrained. Social and physical barriers within cities which limit legitimate spatial behaviour therefore also limit criminal opportunities. Likewise, concentration of channels of access between residence, workplace and social venues may augment opportunities visible from them. This arena is highly under-researched but its potential is indicated by patterns of burglary commission (Brantingham and Brantingham, 1975a, b; Davidson, 1980b) and by criminal networks (Herbert, 1977a, 1979).

(iii) Neighbourhood Effect. The effects of propinquity are reinforced by patterns of social segregation. The wider environment has an influence on patterns of criminal behaviour quite independent to that of individual factors. This so-called neighbourhood effect has been observed most clearly in connection with social class (McDonald, 1969; Baldwin and Bottoms, 1976; Johnstone, 1978; Braithwaite, 1979), but it may also be important in determining patterns of victimisation (Sparks *et al.*, 1977; Hindelang *et al.*, 1978). Much criminal activity is highly localised (Pyle, 1976a; Mawby, 1979b) but little is known about the interaction between simple proximity and the invisible limits placed on behavioural and perhaps more significantly perceptual worlds by the mosaic of urban neighbourhoods. There is a need, moreover, to set journey-to-crime in the wider context of community reactions to crime discussed in Chapter 4.

(iv) Social Mix. Whereas the neighbourhood effect is concerned with the offender's relationship with his social milieu, contrasts between communities are also important. Social mix and social contrast are issues of some debate. Braithwaite (1979) finds some support for the notion that, in Western societies, cities which segregate their poor have higher crime rates, but the evidence is far from unequivocal. On a more local scale, areas with a mixture of housing tenures may also suffer less crime (Davidson, 1976). However, heterogeneity or diversity in social

composition are not necessarily uniformly beneficial. Indeed there may be substantial differences in the effect of social mix between types of residential environment (Baldwin and Bottoms, 1976). The relationship between physical distance and social distance is crucial: sharp social gradients are particularly important for some offence types, for example burglary (Waller and Okihiro, 1978) or robbery (Dean, 1980). Land use mix is also implicated by Jeffery (1976), Newman (1972) and Scarr (1973) in general and particular contexts.

Environment as Opportunity

(a) Predisposing Opportunities

Following the original dichotomy of Morris (1957), predisposing opportunities refer to factors influencing the propensity of individuals to indulge in criminal activity. The scheme laid out here parallels that of Chapter 3 but the discussion is extended to include patterns of victimisation since it is clear that Morris's dichotomy is equally applicable to victims as well as to offenders.

(i) Social Class. Considerable research effort has been devoted over the years to the issue of the effect of social class on crime. Braithwaite (1979) in his exhaustive review of nearly 300 such studies concludes that there are distinct effects for social class of area and social class of individual. For adults the effects are qualified by the restriction that they refer to those types of crime handled by the police: this restriction does not apply to juveniles who are unable to participate in white-collar crime. While there is strong evidence that lower-class people and people from lower-class areas commit more crimes, less is said about the mechanisms of predisposition – how class inequalities may lead to crime. Not that there has been a lack of theorising (Braithwaite, 1979; Glaser, 1979) but rather that the theories are at best partial. Does social class work directly through the acceptance or transmission of particular value systems or indirectly through the environments provided by work, school or leisure activities? The former is less likely since not everyone from a lower-class background or area gets involved in crime. Indeed there can be startling differences in crime rates between areas of similar social status.

From a different perspective, Hindelang (1978) has observed race differences in patterns of victimisation in the United States. Sparks *et al.* (1977) are more cautious of similar conclusions about Britain and find little evidence of class bias in reporting crime in their survey. On the other hand they found some small, but significant, class differences in perceptions of crime, particularly in ratings of seriousness. Working-class people generally perceive property crimes as more and violent crimes as less serious than middle-class people.

What inferences may be drawn from this about the role of social class? On one level it provides a simple and accessible key for highlighting contrasts in patterns of offending and as such it serves a useful purpose in revealing the extent of inequalities which exist. Penetrate beyond this and the facade of social class begins to crumble for it is far from a monolithic concept. Differences in power, income, job security, spending habits, social networks and so on which are subsumed to the notion of social class have varying implications for crime and perhaps more importantly for different types of crime. If the time is ripe for a retreat from the search for all-embracing explanations of crime, then this is an arena in which to begin.

(ii) Housing Class. There is a long tradition of associating crime with poor housing conditions – from the nineteenth century, through the Chicago school to the many recent ecological analyses. In some ways this tradition parallels that of social class though housing has not been regarded as so central a theoretical object. Many of the treatments have taken correlation between crime and housing conditions as peripheral, even coincidental (cf. reviews of ecological analyses by Baldwin (1975a, 1979) and Wilkes (1967)). The particular issue of crowding, however, has been the source of some controversy. Booth *et al.* (1976) attempt to isolate the effects of population density but are severely criticised by Higgins *et al.* (1976). Crowding is set in other contexts by Gillis (1974) and Freedman (1975). The best review is by Roncek (1975).

The role of housing has been given a new thrust by a recent emphasis on tenure arrangements. Its main proponents have come from the Sheffield Study on Urban Social Structure and Crime and cover a wide range of perspectives including differentials in offence and offender rates (Bottoms, 1976; Baldwin and Bottoms, 1976), perceptions (Baldwin, 1974), victimisation (Mawby, 1979a) and policing (Mawby, 1979b). Its roots are seen in the earlier work of Lambert (1970) on Birmingham and in the theoretical analysis of housing initiated by Rex and Moore (1967). A similar, if less penetrating, account of differences between residental environments in the United States is given by Pyle (1976b).

As yet the theoretical implications of tenure arrangements as predisposing factors in crime have not been fully reviewed. Why should renting a house be associated with a greater likelihood of offending? Is the effect direct? – renting as one of a cluster of status-frustration powerlessness symbols. Or is it coincidental? – because offenders are likely to end up in rented accommodation. The utility and dangers of housing class in explanations of crime are comparable to social class but with one important difference. Access to housing, certainly in Britain, is dominated by institutional criteria – the allocation rules of Building Societies and Local Authorities. Housing institutions may therefore play important roles in the formation or maintenance of criminal areas through the differential selection and allocation procedures. 'Problem' council estates have been identified as key elements in the pattern of criminal areas (Morris, 1957; Wilson, 1963; Armstrong and Wilson, 1973; Baldwin, 1975b; Baldwin and Bottoms, 1976; Herbert, 1979). There remains a need to set these observations in a wider context of the housing market and housing policy – not just as a factor in offending but also in the development of social reactions to crime within communities.

(iii) Social Environment. This is an ill-defined arena but one with many ramifications. Neighbourhoods provide the backbone of sub-culture theory by locating proscriptive and prescriptive norms and their interaction. Principal foci for the transmission of value systems outside the home are school (see Hargreaves, 1967), work (Ditton, 1977, 1979) and play – the last most important in informal peer groups (for example, see Ley, 1975). The role of the social environment as a predisposing factor in crime should be integrated with wider value systems. General notions of social solidarity/cohesion, feelings for the community and concerns for the quality of life bear significantly on patterns of offending though the relationships are complex (see Conklin, 1975).

Similar predispositions may be relevant also to patterns of victim isation (Hindelang *et al*., 1978; Sparks *et al*., 1977), and indeed in the exercise of discretion by agents of the justice systems, for example police (Cain, 1973; Mawby, 1979b) and magistrates (Hogarth, 1971). The tangle of relationships between crime and the social environment is most clearly seen in certain types of criminal area considered below under the environment as a label.

(b) Precipitating Opportunities

Precipitating opportunities refer to factors determining the commission of an offence at a particular time and place. Crimes may be precipitated by the victim or target, by the activities of the offender or by the structure of the physical environment.

(i) Targets. A wealth of information exists on victim precipitation, involving both the wider environment and more specific situational factors. For crimes of violence, the type of location has an important bearing on the seriousness of injury (Curtis, 1974; Gottfredson and Hindelang, 1976; Block, 1977). These effects are mediated by the role of privacy and visibility both for the offender and victim: greater violence occurs in private. The use or threat of use of force also varies with the type of location, and there may be significant differences between robbery and straightforward assault (Dunn, 1976a, 1976b). For personal theft without violence, likelihood of loss is greater in more public locations (Hindelang *et al.*, 1978).

The analysis of specific types of crime has revealed the range of precipitating factors. McClintock and Gibson (1961) made an early effort to use a situational classification of robbery in London – later compared to Philadelphia by Normandeau (1969). A similar scheme is used by Lambert (1970) to examine the distribution of minor disputes in Birmingham. Conklin (1976) relates the risks of robbery among the elderly to their fears of victimisation and the constraints this places upon them. Dunn (1976b) considers differences between robberies located in various types of social area. Burglary provides a contrasting set of factors for it is more impersonal and lacks the element of personal confrontation, though its consequence may be just as devastating for the victim. Burglaries tend to be localised (Brantingham and Brantingham, 1975a, b; Davidson, 1980b), if not quite to the extent of crimes of violence, and proximity to areas of offender residence is an important determinant of risks, especially for wealthier districts (Waller and Okihiro, 1978). Wealth itself does not appear to be a vital precipitating factor but vulnerability is (Reppetto, 1974; Davidson, 1980b). Shoplifting is different again (Walsh, 1978) and there are many other types of theft for which the elements of precipitating opportunity remain unidentified. Ley and Cybriwsky's (1974) study of car-stripping gives some indication of the potential in this arena. The situational perspective on crime commission is reviewed by Clarke (1980) who suggests that its utility as a basis for preventive measures has been undervalued.

(ii) Activities. The activities of offenders may precipitate a particular event by bringing an opportunity within range or by placing a unique,

often transient, value on involvement. Belson (1975) finds one of the strongest associations with levels of stealing among London boys is not just the desire for a lot of fun and excitement but the tendency to go out and seek it. Juvenile gangs and informal groups may have an integral crime component but more often offending is a by-product of situations which the group has entered for legal purposes (see Ley (1975) for a review of the spatial ecology of street gangs). An alternative view is that certain activities may precipitate arrest rather than the event itself. Such a possibility is greater for coloured minorities whose visibility may make them more vulnerable to selective police activity. Differences in arrest rates between blacks and whites in London are so great for certain offences, for example being a 'suspected person', that such an explanation cannot be ruled out (Stevens and Willis, 1979). A further topic requiring evaluation within this arena is the extent to which drinking habits precipitate crime for both offenders and victims.

(iii) Physical Environment. The role of features of architecture and design in patterns of crime has been popularised by Oscar Newman (1972) in his theory of defensible space. Essentially this states that certain locations precipitate crime by ambiguities in their definition as private or public space. Streets are recognised as dangerous, behaviour appropriately modified and reactions to crime for victim or witness prescribed by a reliance on the police. Private space, on the other hand, is subject to informal social control through surveillance of residents and potential offenders are inhibited by the likelihood of being recognised as strangers. Reviewers of Newman's ideas (Bottoms, 1974; Reppetto, 1976b; Mawby, 1977b; Mayhew, 1979) have expressed reservations, not so much with the basic concepts, but with their application and implications. As Mawby (1977b) points out, high-rise developments with poor defensible space properties may suffer more crimes of certain types, for example doorstep theft and vandalism but the same design may inhibit burglary by reducing access and escape routes. Likewise, low-rise developments with good defensible space may have higher rates of residential theft because of the greater concealment offered by gardens or greater opportunities offered by residents as a consequence of their feelings of security. There is little doubt about the merits of the physical environment as a source of precipitating opportunity but overarching theory should be eschewed and any analysis thoroughly grounded in a crime-specific approach. Conclusions, however, about the desirability of design features in the prevention of crime will need to accommodate the problem of crime displacement to be

discussed in the final chapter.

Environment as a Label

We have observed considerable differences between places in the incidence of crime, in the concentration of offenders and in patterns of victimisation. There are, similarly, variations between communities in perceptions of crime, feelings of safety and attitudes towards the law and law-breaking. Neighbourhoods play a key role in the integration of these patterns for there is a body of evidence to suggest that the neighbourhood exerts an influence above and independent of individual criteria. In this final section, three alternative conceptualisations of the neighbourhood as a criminal environment are presented. All are extreme forms.

(i) Neighbourhood as a Fortress. Communities which suffer much crime, where fears are great and confidence in the police is low may develop a defence mentality. Homes get made more secure, shop-fronts shuttered and activities curtailed. Legal firearm ownership – an American phenomenon – may be increased (Bordua and Lizotte, 1979). The process spirals as retreat and isolation diminish informal social controls. It may be more exaggerated if the neighbourhood contains a high proportion of people whose fears are greater – women, the elderly or the rich. It can persist even when fears are unrealistically high. The development of fortress neighbourhoods reflects the fact that fear of crime is not simply an expression of anxiety about becoming a victim or of actual victimisation experiences (Garofalo and Laub, 1978). The collective response may dominate the individual (Conklin, 1975).

The defence mentality is equally applicable to offenders. Indeed it may not be realistic to separate offenders and victims in this sort of neighbourhood except by some age and sex differences. Many crimes are highly localised and victims and offenders tend to come from the same class and racial backgrounds. For violence, a high proportion know each other prior to the offence. Communities which adopt a defensive posture towards crime become less active in other areas of interpersonal relations, thereby reducing the potential for integration of offenders within legitimate social networks. The networks themselves become weaker and anonymity increases. It is not surprising, therefore, if patterns of association within criminal networks are strengthened. In addition, defensive responses to crime may lead to escalation of the threat offered as offenders perceive a greater need to use force to achieve their ends. By the same token the police become involved in the vicious circle: in the United States, for example, police use of deadly force is correlated with rates of violence within communities (Kania and Mackey, 1977; Fyfe, 1980). Defended neighbourhoods represent communities whose supportive and responsive functions have atrophied. Their development seems a peculiarly urban phenomenon – a reaction, perhaps, to the scale and anonymity of cities – and crime is not their only problem (Suttles, 1972).

(ii) Neighbourhood as a Refuge. Some communities where crime is perceived as serious and risks are high retain a strong degree of social cohesion. Allied with a tolerance of crime expressed by a lack of support for the law, such communities may develop as a haven for criminal activity. Attitudes in refuge environments express alienation from the general norms of society: crime in these neighbourhoods is not so much a violation of the norm as the norm itself. Demographic structures tend to be more balanced and social networks stronger which may help reduce fears of crime or more specifically of the consequences of crime. Lack of fear, however, can increase the casual opportunities offered for offending by leaving doors unlocked, purses lying about, property unsupervised. The dislocation between acknowledgement that crime is a problem and belief that personal victimisation is unlikely may be general. Moreover, offenders and victims may be strongly intermingled and provide a partial explanation for lack of support for the law. Victims' reluctance to involve the police may be unconnected with the incident, but part of a pre-existing desire to avoid contact with the law. Indeed there is evidence that those unwilling to call the police tend to be more opposed to law violation through their more authoritarian attitudes (Conklin, 1975).

Unlike fortress neighbourhoods, the supportive and responsive roles of the community in refuge environments are strongly developed. The normative role may also be strong, though the norms will be at variance with those accepted elsewhere. Patterns of offending will differ also with a greater emphasis on personal crimes, particularly impulsive violence and petty theft. Again the role of the police may be an integral part of refuge relationships. There is little evidence of differential policing (Mawby, 1979b), but police recording practices may vary between communities reflecting differential perceptions among policemen about their role as law enforcers (Cain, 1973; Sparks *et al.*, 1977; see Table 4.3 and discussion). Likewise, as the case study of Hull reported in Chapter 5 suggests, magistrates' perceptions of refuge environments may influence the distribution of justice particularly for juveniles.

(iii) The Stigmatised Neighbourhood. The stigmatised neighbourhood is the spatial expression of the powerful and prevalent views of criminals as outsiders. Such views are held even when strongly at variance with reality – even the residents of areas with the highest offence and offender rates believe crime is committed by someone from somewhere else (Hindelang *et al.*, 1978). So blame for crime (and other forms of deviance) is projected onto small or weaker groups – a process that is facilitated if the imputed delinquents are easily identified by skin colour or ethnic origin and residential propinquity. Damer (1974) gives a detailed account of how a small slum-clearance housing estate in Glasgow achieved a largely false reputation for deviancy and of how the label became reality as the inhabitants lived up to the expectations imposed upon them. Concurrence of the police or other authority figures in the reputation, however false, only exaggerates the effect (Baldwin, 1974). Similarly tenant selection or self-selection processes may serve to strengthen the neighbourhood's image, particularly in the case of 'problem' council estates in Britain (Wilson, 1963; Herbert, 1979). The origins of the criminal reputations of neighbourhoods are elusive, their basis may be false but their effects are none the less real. The power of the environment as a label should not be ignored, however devious its role.

7 REFLECTIONS

Many of the inferences and conclusions drawn from the material reviewed in this book have clear implications for crime policy. Crimes may be prevented by improving environmental design, by improving security precautions or by reducing vulnerability. Crime levels may be lowered by increasing the supportive and responsive qualities of the neighbourhood through greater social cohesion. Such claims are terribly easy to make but there are inherent dangers. First, as Bottomley (1979) remarks, *understanding* crime is not the same as *controlling* it. The values and assumptions of criminologists who attempt to provide understanding may differ from the police and others who are invested with control. Translation from one ideological realm to another may alter the utility, meaning or consequences of a particular assertion. Secondly, there are serious practical difficulties surrounding policy application of environmental inferences. These focus on the problem of crime displacement – the extent to which offending will be merely transferred to a different place and time. Thirdly, *understanding* crime is not the same as *coping* with it. Crime is a problem because of the difficulties, real, imaginary or anticipated, which people have in coping with it. We need to question the contribution that environmental explanations make in this direction. My intention in concluding this volume is not, therefore, to indicate policy prescriptions, but rather to reflect on these three issues – ideology, displacement and coping with crime – as a preparation for policy evaluation.

Crime, Environment and Ideology

We have observed a wide variety of environmental explanations of crime at different levels. All of these involve implicit ideological assumptions which have so far been ignored. Indeed it may be argued that ideology is the dominant influence on the inferences reached from the evidence we have reviewed, and even on the selection of evidence for review. Theories, explanations, data, prescriptions, policies, solutions – nothing is exempt from the value systems we bring to bear as individuals, laymen or professionals. Any proper evaluation of the utility of theories, etc., therefore requires the ideological assumptions to be made explicit. Four main ideological positions are discussed below. Their outline owes much to the critical reviews of Taylor *et al.* (1973, 1975) although the broader structure of Tulloch (1978) was found useful. The comments made here are selective and no attempt is made to explore the epistemological roots of the various ideologies, nor to present detailed justifications. The emphasis is on the methodological aspects of ideology, that is on the values which underpin views on the utility of environmental factors in crime. These comments are based on an earlier paper which explored the role of values in the assessment of urban crime rates (Davidson, 1980a). See also Peet (1975, 1976) and Harries (1975, 1976b) who debate ideological perspectives on crime.

(a) Conservatism

Conservatism is the dominant ideology of the administrators and servants of the criminal justice system. It stands on the fundamental belief in the natural order of society – in the legitimacy of hierarchy and dominance. Deviants are seen as misfits within the natural order – misfits to be weeded out before they contaminate society's healthy body. Victims are seen as unfortunates who may have contributed to their own downfall through negligence or provocation. Two rather different conservative attitudes to deviancy are connected with views on justice. One is punitive: that in committing a crime an individual forfeits his rights in society – his liberty and even his property. The other is paternalistic: offenders are unfortunate or misguided but as long as there is no danger of further offending, individuals may retain their rights. In a wider sphere, conservatives view the criminal justice system as an instrument of containment, so policy orientations tend to emphasise management rather than elimination of the crime problem.

The conservative's attitude to environmental factors is essentially unproblematic. Accurate description of patterns can be used to improve the efficiency of the relevant part of the criminal justice system. Spatial inequalities no more nor less than wealth or class are part of the accepted natural order. The fact that criminals are concentrated in certain areas is interpreted as 'unfortunate' but if they 'pull themselves together' they may be able to get out. The observation that living in such areas may actually lead to offending is countered by pleas for better education, better housing, better facilities, etc. Conservative arguments for the irrelevance or at least coincidence of environmental factors in crime are extremely difficult to counter given their initial assumptions which, if so narrowly defined as to beg the question, are usually realistic. 'It's a competitive world, somebody has to lose.' But such realism provides us with no explanation nor understanding of the consequences of failure – where failure breeds failure until even the potentially successful are unable to break out of the cycle. Nor can it be assumed that the successful are never deviant.

(b) Liberalism

The liberal position rests on two fundamental conceptions – the explicit recognition of the inequalities in society and the belief that they can be rectified. The key to the liberal approach is knowledge – the premiss that knowledge leads to understanding and understanding to prevention or cure. So liberals will wish to prescribe as well as describe. Most of the studies reviewed in this volume are predicated explicitly or implicitly upon these assumptions, so liberalism may be identified as the dominant ideology among criminologists, as it is among social workers and other agents of social control on the periphery of the criminal justice system. Three rather different, but overlapping, traditions inspire the liberal stance. The reformist school concentrates on the overhaul of the criminal justice system to ensure that it becomes more effective or humane. Positivism emphasises the rehabilitative role of the criminal justice system. Offenders are seen as unwilling victims of circumstances beyond their control (of which environment is but one among personality, upbringing, life experiences, social pressures, biological necessities, etc.). With treatment and support re-offending can be prevented and the offender restored to a normal functioning role in society. The third tradition is more nebulous: it revolves round romantic, idealistic or benevolent beliefs in the common good. Unlike the conservative's use of consensus as a means of investing the views of a privileged elite on the majority, liberals believe in the inherent right of majority views to prevail, and the consensus is seen as a final arbiter. Deviant minorities must conform in the interests of the majority. And yet while most liberals reject moral appeals in favour of objectivity and rationality, notions of a social conscience, the terms of which are rarely explicitly or implicitly defined, form a mainspring of intellectual and practical effort.

Environmental factors are an essential prerequisite of most liberal explanations of criminal behaviour and indeed there is widespread recognition of environmental prescriptions in solving some of the problems of crime. The key role is the identification of criminal areas. Identify these, and we can identify the individuals in need of treatment and concentrate supportive resources. Area-based policies in education, housing and job-creation have received a measure of official recognition: efforts on crime remain sporadic and unco-ordinated despite its significance as an element in the quality of life.

Criticism has been levelled at the liberal position on a number of grounds. It has been deemed to have inspired a retreat to individualism – a mechanistic search for the combination of factors which gives the best predictions of rates of criminal offending. What is not made explicit is that such factors – poor housing, overcrowding, unemployment, proximity to delinquent opportunities, etc. – may themselves be just as much an outcome of deeper social processes as the crime rate. The focus is on immediate circumstances rather than root cause. Liberal claims to objectivity are a further source of criticism. Statistical sophistication and purity have become ends in themselves, obscuring the meaning of results or, when applied to dubious data, obscuring the validity of the whole exercise. In other cases, objectivity is used as an excuse for opting out of any form of substantial conclusion on the grounds that it is self-evident. Indeed excessive empiricism is a continuing weakness. Theory is often patchy or incoherent, questions of relevance are ignored and the pursuit of technical expertise allowed to dominate substantive findings. The ecological analysis of crime rates is an example of an approach where many of these criticisms are valid (Baldwin, 1975a). And yet however well-founded the scepticism of liberal efforts, it should not be allowed to obscure the real progress which has been made in unravelling the complex and varied links between crime and environment.

(c) Radicalism

The radical assumes the primacy of man (rather than of the social system) and his social nature. Conflict rather than consensus is seen as the major factor in the allocation of societal resources. Social justice is measured in terms of equality of average outcomes in the allocative process rather than the liberal criterion of equality of access. Crime is regarded as a product of social relations – of the interactions between individuals with different value systems. Definitions of crime are not an inherent quality of an act, but are imposed by the actors and depend on who the actor is, offender, victim or policeman, etc. Where liberalism entails a descent to individualism, radicalism involves locating individuals and events within their social setting and emphasising the role of the community in defining crime and its consequences. Thus the community gives a context to crime commission and sets the standards of response or reaction. Radicals believe in practice as well as description and prescription – that knowledge can only properly come from involvement and can only properly be used with involvement. Nothing is value-free.

From the radical perspective, environmental factors are seen as an essential but unique and passive backdrop to individual actions and motivations. The setting may mediate the transactions between individuals but not control their shape or form. Definitions and meanings may vary with the environmental situation of the act, but primacy is given to the actors' role relationships. A more hard-line view would be that physical and social environments are no less subject than any other element in the act to manipulation in the actors' struggle for dominance.

The major criticism of radicalism is that excessive emphasis is devoted to 'victimless' crimes, such as drug-taking or prostitution, and that it has little to offer on property offences which dominate patterns of offending, however defined. This emphasis arises from the dominant ethnocentric viewpoint of radicalism and its predisposition to reject second-hand evidence, whether official records or informal accounts. First-hand knowledge, however, through participant observation or direct experience is not easily achieved in the sporadic, spontaneous and sanctionable activity which constitutes most crime. The validity of radical theory as provided by the labelling or transactionalist perspectives is not itself questioned, but rather the value of its application to a range of events to which its criteria are not so relevant. At the same time, we have observed that labelling occurs at neighbourhood or community level in a variety of guises so its potential if limited is far from exhausted.

(d) Socialism

Many of the basic assumptions are shared with radicalism – primacy of man, his social nature, need to integrate knowledge and action, pervasiveness of values. However, there are some significant points of departure. While accepting the need to understand value systems, socialists recognise that values are historically specific. Laws may be outmoded or obsolete, so definitions of crime should be located in the social relations dominant at the time of the introduction of the laws governing that activity. More important a distinction from radicalism is the socialist emphasis on property relations: crime is an outcome of the property-based class distinctions of capitalist society. Indeed, crime is regarded as a necessary part of the legitimation of capitalist power structures. So explanations of property crime are more readily accommodated by the socialist argument. As with liberals and radicals, there is an explicit recognition of the inequalities in society. Unlike them socialists are committed to the abolition of inequality through a restructuring of society rather than its rectification through more powerful social policy.

Socialists view the environment as an inequality generated by other inequalities. The organisation of space, physical or social, is an instrument of class domination, one form of control exerted by the powerful over the weak. Environmental factors are therefore regarded as at worst irrelevant or at best instrumental but subordinate to crime seen as emanating directly from the social formation.

One area of contradiction within the socialist position is the relation between societal and individual levels of analysis. For example, the debate about equality (of total outcomes at societal level) and diversity (accommodation of different pursuits at individual level) is so far weakly resolved. Class conflict at societal level provides a rationale for the existence of crime, but such explanations tend to diminish the fact that many crimes are highly localised, intra-class events with, in the case of violence, a high chance of the participants knowing each other. The assertion that the abolition of property relations will remove crime ignores the fact that there are other sources of conflict in interpersonal relations, for example in sex roles or expressions of personality. Nor does it admit the possibility of other forms of abuse replacing theft. The socialist perspective on crime has merit arising from the integration of thought and action, from its desire to make explicit the ideological frame and from its efforts to set theory in a proper historical context. Yet its latent power is perhaps unrealised as its debates have tended to be rather polemical and give undue emphasis to criticism.

(e) Ideological Attrition

The conclusion to be drawn from this review of alternative ideological perspectives is that to place any degree of significance on environmental factors in crime is to take a mainstream liberal stance. The greater the departure in either direction, the more irrelevant the environment is regarded. But strictly the positions merely inform interpretations: the subject of interpretation, for example the environment, is available to any ideological realm. Socialists (and radicals, for they do not differ substantially on this) regard subject and object of enquiry as inseparable from interpretation, so in this sense their position is most complete. Conservatives on the other hand are more disposed to pragmatic shifts as long as these serve the *status quo* so tend to regard full accounts as an encumbrance. Move a concept, axiom, theory or conclusion from any realm towards conservatism and if not rejected outright it will suffer ideological attrition as parts of the interpretation are rendered irrelevant. Movement towards radicalism/socialism is rare since rejection is likely on the grounds of inadequacy or incompleteness. Movement is important because of the functional separation and ideological differences between on the one hand criminologists who are concerned with providing understanding of crime and criminal behaviour and, on the other, the servants of the penal system who are delegated responsibility for controlling it.

To illustrate the problem of ideological attrition, let us briefly reconsider the theory of defensible space (Newman, 1972). It would be hard to deny that Newman's work is thoroughly in the liberal tradition. All the hall-marks are there – objective evaluation of empirical data, emphasis on patterns of individual events, description plus prescription. We may accept the views of his critics that defensible space is not so widely applicable as Newman's analysis suggested, but the lessons for crime prevention remain clear. Indeed Newman went on to propose guidelines for incorporating defensive space properties in urban renewal projects (Newman, 1975) accommodating some of the criticism. Move defensible space theory into the hands of those responsible for operating policies, however, and it becomes a selective instrument for social control. Selection will be based on the allocation of scarce resources and perceptions of need for control. For the police, this could mean additional patrols in areas suggested by the theory, or increased electronic surveillance. However, resources will inevitably limit the extent of such measures, leaving other areas and the basis of the problem untouched. More insidiously, greater reliance on the police does not appear to lead to a reduction in crime: indeed it may lead to more crime as it is accompanied by retreat, isolation and lack of community support. For architects, defensible space is relatively cheap for new projects, but impossibly expensive for existing projects that lack it. Even with new projects, a choice exists about how much defensible space at what cost. Scarce resources dictate that full application of defensible space ideas is only possible as a premium on selected new high income projects which are unlikely to be built in the vicinity of criminal areas where the need is greatest. Whatever potency the theory has can, therefore, be considerably diminished by translation from liberal to conservative realms.

A further example of the potential for emasculation by ideological attrition is community policing. The theory is again largely liberal in origin: it suggests that the effectiveness of policing may be improved by placing policemen in the community, not so much to catch criminals as to open up channels of communication and increase confidence in the police through being known and recognised. The notion of community policing arose from fears that the modern, technologically-equipped, car-based patrol was weakening the links between policemen and their main source of information – the public. It was also being observed – among policemen (see for example Alderson, 1979) as well as criminologists (for example, Mawby, 1979b) – that the bulk of police time is not spent catching criminals nor are most criminals apprehended as a direct consequence of police activity. Placing the policeman back in the community especially in high crime areas would, therefore, also serve as a catalyst for improving the supportive and responsive elements in the community response to crime and so diminishing the chances of withdrawal into the fortress mentality with consequential deterioration of social life. Whatever the merits and demerits of community policing in theory, problems of a rather different nature may arise in operationalising it. These are illustrated in Schaffer's account of one aspect of community policing – a juvenile liaison experiment in Glasgow (Schaffer, 1980, Chapter 2). The project involved the use of unit beat officers in the supervision of young offenders. After some initial hostility the scheme was felt to be a success by most of the supervisory beat officers, by the juveniles and their families, and by other social workers. It failed to gain the support of the middle-rank policemen responsible for its adminstration since its image did not fit easily with traditional policework, in particular the criterion of arrest as a measure of success. This heightened the conflict felt by the supervising officers between their policework and social work roles. Any community policing project will be in danger of failure unless the ideological shift from theoretical premiss to operational criterion is accommodated.

These two rather different examples are selected without particular justification to illustrate the need for awareness of the role of value systems. Other areas of criminal activity where environmental factors, whether community or situation, are relevant could equally bear scrutiny. We have seen that interpersonal violence appears to be mediated, certainly in the degree of injury, by its location. Attempts to control wife-battering will have a rather different ideological bias from attempts to understand it. Theft, likewise, has locational significance relevant to policy – how to protect against burglary, how to control shoplifting or employee theft, etc. – but again prescriptions need to be protected from ideological attrition.

The Problem of Displacement

We have suggested in Chapters 3 and 6 that for a wide range of crimes the immediate circumstance or situation of an offence has important bearing on its incidence and on its consequences. Specific victimisations depend, therefore, on the convergence of predispositions among potential offenders (their propensity to commit crimes, their likelihood to be in a particular place at a particular time) and precipitation offered by potential victims or targets (visibility, attractiveness, vulnerability, provocation). If many crimes are opportunistic in this way, then an understanding of situation or circumstance has direct implication for crime prevention (Clarke, 1980). Reduce opportunities and crime will be reduced. The last decade has seen a growing interest in such an approach but it suffers from a major drawback – the problem of crime displacement. Reduction of opportunity in one situation may simply result in another victim being chosen elsewhere or at another time when circumstances are more favourable. No crime policy based on opportunity theory can be successful without a thorough evaluation of the displacement problem so that its effects may be mitigated or avoided. To date, investigations of displacement have been patchy and inconclusive: and there are some formidable measurement problems.

(a) Types of Displacement

Displacement may take place in different ways (Reppetto, 1976a; Clarke, 1980; Hough *et al.*, 1980). The effect may be quite straightforward, but measurement difficulties are most acute when more than one form of displacement is involved.

(i) Time. Deferment is a very common form of displacement. It happens when something alters the potential offender's perception of the favourability of particular circumstances, for example a change in policing methods or other form of social control. Saturation policing suffers from this form of displacement: Dean (1980) recounts how street robbery in the Brixton area of London declined rapidly during a period of intense activity by the Metropolitan Police's Special Patrol Group, but rose rapidly again thereafter. Likewise, reducing truancy by employing more school attendance officers or special patrols may have limited impact on juvenile crime if the offenders displace their

offending to the evening hours (that is, if it has any impact at all – the truancy issue may not be that straightforward – see Ekblom, 1980). Temporary deferment will reduce the level of crime in a given period (if only by displacing some of it into the next period) without the need to tackle any of the underlying causes of crime. To achieve a worthwhile reduction may require substantial resources: there may also, in the case of saturation policing, be unintended side effects especially in refuge environments in reducing respect and support for the law.

(ii) Method. This type of displacement occurs when a different means is used to achieve the same end. Thwarted by installation of alarms, business burglars may resort to smash and grab. Bank robbers unable to force the modern high-technology safe turn to weapons-assisted snatches of cash in transit. Displacement of this type suggests a high level of motivation on the part of the offender towards a particular target – one of the key characteristics of the 'professional' criminal for whom situational prevention measures are likely to be rather less effective.

(iii) Type of Crime. Reducing the opportunities for one form of criminal activity may result in displacement to another. Shoplifters may turn to vandalism, burglars to mugging. It has been suggested that this form of displacement is limited by the association between types of crime and the personality of offenders (Reppetto, 1974, 1976a): burglars do not like confronting their victim, robbers prefer confrontation to stealth. As with displacement of method, changing the type of offence is more likely among individuals highly motivated towards crime for the rewards it brings. On the other hand, offenders whose commitment to crime is low but not specific (those who offend for social reasons, for example peer status acquisition, or for psychological reasons such as self-assertion or loneliness) may more readily transfer to a different form of activity.

(iv) Place. Blocking opportunities in one place may simply shift the attention of offenders to similar targets elsewhere. This is the prime danger of defensible space theory since all targets cannot be equally protected. Reppetto (1976a) concludes that territorial displacement is the most likely form of displacement, particularly as a response to target hardening. However, the potential for territorial displacement is limited by the highly localised nature of much criminal activity. Targets are selected from those visible within the behavioural world of the

offender and this is highly constrained – the more so for juveniles. An illustration of geographical displacement is given in a study of the effects of installing closed-circuit television in certain stations of the London Underground (Burrows, 1980). There is evidence to suggest that some crimes (thefts but not necessarily robberies) were displaced to neighbouring stations. If the observed effects were indeed displacement, 85 per cent of the savings in theft at the stations covered by CCTV would be nullified.

(b) Implications of Foreclosure

Foreclosing opportunities is an attractive means of crime prevention: it is simple, direct and not always expensive. The question is how far is the problem of displacement likely to negate it. A pessimistic answer would be almost completely: the propensity to offend is inelastic and some means of offending will eventually be found. No doubt this is true of highly motivated and skilled offenders but there is good reason to suggest that the majority of offences are petty and not committed by people addicted to crime as a way of life. For example, among residential burglaries in Christchurch, New Zealand (Davidson, 1980b) there is little to indicate planning and premeditation. Rather the reverse, for a majority of burglars used no force for entry and the amount stolen was not significantly greater for those who did (indeed a substantial majority stole nothing or very little). Moreover, burglary in Christchurch is remarkably localised for a low-density city with high car-ownership (see Figure 2.4). In these circumstances, reducing vulnerability, even by such simple expedients as locking doors and windows, is likely to reduce the incidence of burglary. Whether it reduces the overall incidence of crime if other vulnerable targets still exist, is another matter.

There are dangers in foreclosure. If offenders are highly motivated, displacement may be accompanied by an escalation in the means of force used to achieve the end. For example, Ball *et al.* (1978) suggest that improved security measures by banks have been accompanied by greater use of violence by robbers. Expressive violence, on the other hand, has rather limited displacement potential: curtailing minor infractions may lead to rarer, but more serious incidents. But perhaps the greatest danger is partial foreclosure, for if only some of the targets are protected, risks for the remainder will grow. A graphic illustration is the introduction of car-steering locks (Mayhew *et al.*, 1980). In Britain this requirement was applied to new cars only from 1971: the overall rate of car theft and unauthorised taking dipped for a short time then recovered with risks for older vehicles doubling. In the German Federal Republic, the regulation was applied to all cars from 1963: the rate dipped and remained low with risks about one-quarter their previous level. The London Underground closed-circuit television experiment already discussed (Burrows, 1980) also suffered from partiality, the effects of which would be reinforced by the likelihood that many of the individuals deterred from offending at a CCTV-covered station would as Underground users pass through other stations not covered.

While foreclosure of opportunity is commonly regarded as most relevant to the physical elements of the crime situation, it is worth noting that it may be equally applied to the behaviour of victims. Indeed avoiding situations perceived as risky is our first recourse in face of the crime problem. In so doing we come up against a different form of foreclosure – that of normal legitimate activities. Those who have more to fear – the elderly, women, residents of high-crime areas – have the greater erosion of the quality of their lives. So policies which improve the safety of the environment will have tangible benefits for the community at large, not just for the few who may avoid victimisation.

In conclusion, displacement is a pervasive, but variable phenomenon. It is a significant disadvantage of policies which seek to reduce opportunities for crime through the manipulation of environmental factors. Expensive or time-consuming solutions may find themselves partly or wholly vitiated by the effects of displacement. It is a drawback, too, of the crime-specific approach which has been advocated elsewhere in this book as an alternative to the search for all-embracing theories of crime. The value of crime-specific studies will be undermined if the interactions between different types of crime implied by some forms of displacement are ignored. Yet there is cause for optimism. The opportunist and localised nature of many crimes suggests that there are distinct limits to offending especially among the majority whose motivation is weaker and crimes less serious (professional, skilled or determined offenders will be rather less deterred by blocked opportunities). Optimism apart, environmental crime prevention will not come of age until the problem of displacement is properly resolved.

Coping With Crime

It would be hard to argue against the benefits of controlling crime. The direct consequences of crime in terms of injury and property loss are considerable and behind the bald statistics lie less tangible effects in terms of trauma and erosion of the fabric of social life. The costs of control in maintaining a sophisticated criminal justice system are high. There are, therefore, formidable reasons for seeking a reduction in crime and its impact. But has the drive to achieve this seemingly legitimate goal diverted attention from the fact that crime has to be coped with?

Mainstream criminology, and no less within a narrower focus on environmental factors, has interpreted its role in terms of providing explanations. The prime target has been the offender: understand why he offends and (in positivist terms) he may be prevented. Penologists have responded by introducing increasingly sophisticated and individualistic control measures. Has the strategy been successful? In terms of controlling the propensity to offend, the answer is largely no. There is little evidence to suggest that rehabilitation is any more or less effective than traditional penal measures (Lipton *et al.*, 1975; Brody, 1976). This is not to devalue other merits (and demerits) of penal policies (for a review of these see Bottomley, 1979) but their impact on levels of crime appears minimal. In the face of increasing criticism of offender-based explanations, attention is moving to the offence and its circumstances (Clarke, 1980). How is this likely to fare? A little better, perhaps, on the assumption that displacement is not too serious a problem. But foreclosure is not a limitless possibility, so the core of the problem will remain, although there may be debate on its size. Whether the emphasis is on offenders or offences, therefore, the possibility of reducing the impact of crime by reducing crime itself seems to have distinctly finite limits.

If coping with crime is decidedly less attractive a proposition than controlling it, there are nevertheless real benefits to be gained. The issue needs to be tackled on two fronts: coping with prospective fears of victimisation and coping with the consequences. In both, social environment plays a crucial role. For victims the consequences include not just injury or material loss or even the trauma of the event itself, but hidden costs that subsequent involvement with the criminal justice system entails, visits to police station, court, etc. And these may be spread over some time. Victimisation surveys indicate that these are material considerations in the decision to report crime (Sparks *et al.*, 1977; Hindelang *et al.*, 1978). In addition there are variations between communities in norms of victim response, and indeed within communities between different types of crime. As we observed in Chapter 4 the community plays an important role in determining the level of crime and its impact. Strengthen the community's supportive and responsive functions and the impact of crime is diminished as victims are better able to cope. Crime itself, at least in the official sense, may actually be reduced by lower levels of reporting as less need is felt for recourse to the police. Moreover, members of an integrated, cohesive community with a well-defined response to crime may be less inclined to offend. What is needed is a thorough evaluation of the immediate consequences of victimisation and the extent to which individual reactions are rooted in the more general social reaction.

Prospective fears of victimisation are a more delicate issue. While everyone, at some time or another, is motivated by fear of crime, and most people have well-formed opinions on the matter, the nature of the relationship between general fears and the pattern of crime is elusive (Baumer, 1978). At least we know a distinction should be made between general fears or concern about crime and anxieties about becoming a victim of a specific crime (Garofalo and Laub, 1978). We have also seen that projection onto outsiders is a common coping response to perceived crime problems and that this can have repercussions in terms of an area's acquisition of a criminal reputation. In addition, communities vary in their expectations of the police, as do police interpretations of their role *vis-à-vis* the community. The social reaction to crime is formed not just as a response to information from diverse sources, the media, second-hand reports, experience with the police, etc., but as an ongoing dynamic process in which the community plays a vital role as mediator, both between individuals and society and between crime and other social problems. The nature of this role in coping with crime needs to be clarified.

Environments are important, therefore, not only in terms of physical setting, but also of social location. Offences occur in particular places and the characteristics of these make a significant contribution to our understanding. Offenders are concentrated in certain localities which have bearing on why and where they offend. Throughout the criminal justice process, social location is relevant in the formation of perceptions, attitudes and responses to the problem of crime. The environment is emerging as a candidate for remedial action, particularly in crime prevention policies. But it is in the community that our understanding must ultimately be located, for it is the community which sets the standards in defining what is crime (in the practical rather than legalistic sense), which gives context to its commission and which shares with victims the responsibility for coping with its consequences.

BIBLIOGRAPHY

Alderson, J. (1979) *Policing Freedom*, Plymouth: Macdonald and Evans

Amir, M. (1971) *Patterns in Forcible Rape*, Chicago: University of Chicago Press

Ardrey, R. (1966) *The Territorial Imperative*, New York: Atheneum

Armstrong, G. and Wilson, M. (1973) 'Delinquency and Some Aspects of Housing' in C. Ward (ed.), *Vandalism*, London: Architectural Press, pp. 64-84

Aromaa, K. (1974) 'Victimization to Violence: A Gallup Survey', *International Journal of Criminology and Penology, 2*, 333-46

Bagley, C. (1965) 'Juvenile Delinquency in Exeter: An Ecological and Comparative Study', *Urban Studies, 2*, 33-50

Baldwin, J. (1972) 'A Critique of "Delinquent Schools in Tower Hamlets"', *British Journal of Criminology, 12*, 399-401

—— (1974) 'Problem Housing Estates – Perceptions of Tenants, City Officials and Criminologists', *Social and Economic Administration, 8*, 16-35

—— (1975a) 'British Areal Studies of Crime: An Assessment', *British Journal of Criminology, 15*, 211-27

—— (1975b) 'Urban Criminality and the Problem Estate', *Local Government Studies, 1*, 12-20

—— (1979) 'Ecological and Areal Studies in Great Britain and the United States' in N. Morris and M. Tonry (eds.), *Crime and Justice: an Annual Review of Research*, Chicago: University of Chicago Press, pp. 29-66

Baldwin, J. and Bottoms, A.E. (1976) *The Urban Criminal*, London: Tavistock

Ball, J., Chester, L. and Perrott, R. (1978) *Cops and Robbers: An Investigation into Armed Bank Robbery*, London: André Deutsch

Ball, J.C., Ross, A. and Simpson, A. (1964) 'Incidence and Estimated Prevalence of Recorded Delinquency in a Metropolitan Area', *American Sociological Review, 29*, 90-4

Bamisaiye, A. (1974) 'The Spatial Distribution of Juvenile Delinquency and Adult Crime in the City of Ibadan', *International Journal of Criminology and Penology, 2*, 65-83

Banton, M. (1964) *The Policeman in the Community*, London: Tavistock

Barr, H. and O'Leary, E. (1966) *Trends and Regional Comparisons in Probation*, Home Office Research Unit Report No. 8, London: HMSO

Basilevsky, A. (1975) 'Social Class and Delinquency in London Boroughs', *Social Indicators Research, 2*, 287-313

Batta, I.D., McCulloch, J.W. and Smith, N.J. (1975) 'A Study of Juvenile Delinquency Amongst Asians and Half-Asians', *British Journal of Criminology, 15*, 32-42

Baumer, T.L. (1978) 'Research on Fear of Crime in the United States', *Victimology, 3*, 254-64

Becker, H. (1963) *Outsiders*, New York: Free Press

Belson, W.A. (1975) *Juvenile Theft: the Causal Factors*, London: Harper and Row

Black, D.J. (1970) 'Production of Crime Rates', *American Sociological Review, 35*, 733-48

Block, R. (1977) *Violent Crime*, Lexington, Mass.: Lexington Books

Boggs, S.L. (1965) 'Urban Crime Patterns', *American Sociological Review, 30*, 899-908

—— (1971) 'Formal and Informal Crime Control: An Exploratory Study of Urban, Suburban and Rural Orientations', *The Sociological Quarterly, 12*, 319-27

Booth, A., Welch, S. and Johnson, D.R. (1976) 'Crowding and Urban Crime Rates', *Urban Affairs Quarterly, 11*, 291-307, 317-22

Booth, C. (1891) *Life and Labour of the People*, London: Williams and Norgate

Bordua, D.J. (1958) 'Juvenile Delinquency and "anomie": An Attempt at Replication', *Social Problems, 6*, 230-8

Bordua, D.J. and Lizotte, A.J. (1979) 'Patterns of Legal Firearm Ownership: A Cultural and Situational Analysis of Illinois Counties', *Law and Policy Quarterly, 1*, 147-75

Bottomley, A.K. (1973) *Decisions in the Penal Process*, London: Martin Robertson

—— (1979) *Criminology in Focus: Past Trends and Future Prospects*, London: Martin Robertson

Bottomley, A.K. and Coleman, C.A. (1976) 'Criminal Statistics: The Police Role in the Discovery and Detection of Crime', *International Journal of Criminology and Penology, 4*, 33-58

Bottoms, A.E. (1967) 'Delinquency Among Immigrants', *Race, 8*, 357-o3

—— (1974) Review of *Defensible Space* by O. Newman, *British Journal of Criminology, 14*, 203-6

——(1976) 'Crime in a City', *New Society*, 8 April, 164-6

Braithwaite, J. (1979) *Inequality, Crime and Public Policy*, London: Routledge & Kegan Paul

Brantingham, P.J. and Brantingham, P.L. (1975a) 'The Spatial Patterning of Burglary', *Howard Journal, 14*, 11-23

—— (1975b) 'Residential Burglary and Urban Form', *Urban Studies, 12*, 273-84

Brody, S.R. (1976) *The Effectiveness of Sentencing*, Home Office Research Studies No. 35, London: HMSO

Brown, M.J., McCulloch, J.W. and Hiscox, J. (1972) 'Criminal Offences in an Urban Area and Their Associated Social Variables', *British Journal of Criminology, 12*, 250-68

Burrows, J. (1980) 'Closed Circuit Television and Crime on the London Underground' in R.V.G. Clarke and P. Mayhew (eds.), *Designing out Crime*, London: HMSO, pp. 75-83

Burt, C. (1925) *The Young Delinquent*, London: University of London Press

Cain, M. (1973) *Society and the Policeman's Role*, London: Routledge & Kegan Paul

Calhoun, J.B. (1962a) 'Population Density and Social Pathology', *Scientific American, 206*, 139-48

—— (1962b) 'A "Behavioral Sink" ' in E.L. Bliss (ed.), *Roots of Behavior*, New York: Harper

—— (1966) 'The Role of Space in Animal Sociology', *Journal of Social Issues, 22*, 46-58

Carter, R.L. and Hill, K.Q. (1976) 'Criminals' Image of the City and Urban Crime Patterns', *Social Science Quarterly, 57*, 597-607

—— (1979) *The Criminal's Image of the City*, New York: Pergamon Press

Castle, I.M. and Gittus, E. (1957) 'The Distribution of Social Defects in Liverpool', *Sociological Review, 5*, 43-64

Chambliss, W.J. (1975) 'The Political Economy of Crime: A Comparative Study of Nigeria and U.S.A.' in I. Taylor *et al*. (eds.), *Critical Criminology*, London: Routledge & Kegan Paul, pp. 167-80

Chilton, R.J. (1964) 'Continuity in Delinquency Area Research: A Comparison of Studies for Baltimore, Detroit and Indianapolis', *American Sociological Review, 29*, 71-83

Cicourel, A.V. (1976) *The Social Organisation of Juvenile Justice*, (rev. edn), London: Heinemann

Clark, J.P. and Wenninger, E.P. (1962) 'Socio-economic Class and Area as Correlates of Illegal Behavior among Juveniles', *American Socio-*

logical Review, 27, 826-34

Clarke, R.V.G. (1980) ' "Situational" Crime Prevention: Theory and Practice', *British Journal of Criminology, 20*, 136-47

Cloward, R.A. and Ohlin, L.E. (1960) *Delinquency and Opportunity*, New York: Free Press

Cohen, A.K. (1955) *Delinquent Boys: The Culture of the Gang*, New York: Free Press

Coleman, C.A. and Bottomley, A.K. (1976) 'Police Conceptions of Crime and "No Crime" ', *Criminal Law Review*, June 344-60

Conklin, J.E. (1971) 'Dimensions of Community Response to the Crime Problem', *Social Problems, 18*, 373-85

—— (1975) *The Impact of Crime*, New York: Macmillan

—— (1976) 'Robbery, the Elderly and Fear: An Urban Problem in Search of a Solution' in J. Goldsmith and S.S. Goldsmith (eds.), *Crime and the Elderly*, Lexington, Mass.: Lexington Books, pp. 99-110

Conklin, J.E. and Bittner, E. (1973) 'Burglary in a Suburb', *Criminology, 11*, 206-32

Corsi, T.M. and Harvey, M.E. (1975) 'The Socio-economic Determinants of Crime in the City of Cleveland', *Tijdschrift voor Economische en Sociale Geografie, 66*, 323-36

Curtis, L.A. (1974) *Criminal Violence: National Patterns and Behaviour*, Lexington, Mass.: Lexington Books

Damer, S. (1974) 'Wine Alley: The Sociology of a Dreadful Enclosure', *Sociological Review, 22*, 221-48

David, P.R. and Scott, J.W. (1973) 'A Cross-cultural Comparison of Juvenile Offenders, Offenses, Due Processes, and Societies: The Cases of Toledo, Ohio and Rosario, Argentina', *Criminology, 11*, 183-205

Davidson, R.N. (1976) 'Crime and the Urban Environment', paper presented to Section E of the British Association, Lancaster

—— (1977) 'Spatial Bias in Court Sentencing', paper presented to Urban Studies Group, Institute of British Geographers, Leicester

—— (1980a) 'Environment and Ideology: Alternative Perspectives on Urban Crime Rates' in P. Forer (ed.), *Futures in Human Geography*, Christchurch, New Zealand: New Zealand Geographical Society, pp. 27-40

—— (1980b) 'Patterns of Residential Burglary in Christchurch', *New Zealand Geographer, 36*, 73-8

Davidson, R.N. and Francis, M.K. (1973) *Kingston-upon-Hull and Haltemprice: Social Area Analysis*, Part II Commentary, University of Hull, Department of Geography, Miscellaneous Series No. 15

Dean, M. (1980) 'The Other Side of the Tracks', *Guardian*, 19

November

Ditton, J. (1977) *Part-time Crime: An Ethnography of Fiddling and Pilferage*, London: Macmillan

—— (1979) *Controlology: Beyond the New Criminology*, London, Macmillan

Doerner, W.G. (1975) 'A Regional Analysis of Homicide Rates in the United States', *Criminology, 13*, 90-101

Douglas, J.W.B., Ross, J.M., Hammond W.A. and Mulligan,D.G. (1966) 'Delinquency and Social Class', *British Journal of Criminology, 6*, 294-302

Dunn, C.S. (1976a) *The Pattern and Distribution of Assault Incident Characteristics among Social Areas*, Utilization of Criminal Statistics Project, Analytic Report No. 14, Washington: US Government Printing Office

—— (1976b) *Patterns of Robbery Characteristics and their Occurrence among Social Areas*, Utilization of Criminal Statistics Project, Analytic Report No 15, Washington: US Government Printing Office

Durant, M., Thomas, M. and Willcock, H.D. (1972) *Crime, Criminals and the Law*, London: HMSO

Ealand, C.P.H. (1976) *Diving off the Deep End*, London: Release Publications

Edwards, A. (1973) 'Sex and Area Variations in Delinquency Rates in an English City', *British Journal of Criminology, 13*, 121-37

Ekblom, P. (1980) 'Police Truancy Patrols' in R.V.G. Clarke and P. Mayhew (eds.), *Designing out Crime*, London: HMSO, pp. 85-98

Ennis, P.H. (1967) *Criminal Victimization in the United States*, Field Surveys II of th President's Commission on Law Enforcement and Administration of Justice, NORC, University of Chicago

Evans, D.J. (1980) *Geographical Perspectives on Juvenile Delinquency*, Farnborough: Gower

FBI (annual) *Uniform Crime Reports for the United States*, Washington: US Government Printing Office

Fischer, C.S., Baldassare, M. and Ofshe, R.J. (1975) 'Crowding Studies and Urban Life: A Critical Review', *Journal of the American Institute of Planners, 41*, 406-18

Fishman, G. (1979) 'Patterns of Victimization and Notification', *British Journal of Criminology, 19*, 146-57

Freedman, J.L. (1972) 'Population Density, Juvenile Delinquency and Mental Illness in New York City' in S.M. Mazie (ed.), *Commission on Population Growth and the American Future*, Research Report

Volume V, Washington: US Government Printing Office, pp. 512-23

——(1975) *Crowding and Behavior*, San Francisco: Freeman

Fyfe, J.J. (1980) 'Geographic Correlates of Police Shooting: A Micro-analysis', *Journal of Research in Crime and Delinquency, 17*, 101-13

Galle, O.R., Gove, W. and McPherson, J.M. (1972) 'Population Density and Pathology', *Science, 176* (7 April), 23-30

Garofalo, J. and Laub, J. (1978) 'The Fear of Crime: Broadening our Perspective', *Victimology, 3*, 242-53

Gastil, R.D. (1972) 'Homicide and a Regional Culture of Violence', *American Sociological Review, 36*, 412-27

Gelles, R.J. (1979) *Family Violence*, Beverley Hills: Sage

Giggs, J.A. (1970) 'Socially Disorganised Areas in Barry: A Multivariate Analysis' in H. Carter and W.K.D. Davies (eds.), *Urban Essays: Studies in the Geography of Wales*, London: Longman

Gillis, A.R. (1974) 'Population Density and Social Pathology: The Case of Building Type, Social Allowance and Juvenile Delinquency', *Social Forces, 53*, 306-14

Glaser, D. (1962) 'The Differential-association Theory of Crime' in A.M. Rose (ed.), *Human Behaviour and Social Processes*, London: Routledge & Kegan Paul

—— (1979) 'A Review of Crime-causation Theory and Its Application' in N. Morris and M. Tonry (eds.), *Crime and Justice: An Annual Review of Research*, Chicago: University of Chicago Press, pp. 203-37

Gordon, R.A. (1967) 'Issues in the Ecological Study of Delinquency', *American Sociological Review, 32*, 927-44

Gottfredson, M.R. and Hindelang, M.J. (1976) 'Bodily Injury in Personal Crimes' in W.G. Skogan (ed.), *Sample Surveys of the Victims of Crime*, Cambridge, Mass.: Ballinger, pp. 73-87

Green, E. (1961) *Judicial Attitudes in Sentencing: A Study of the Factors Underlying the Sentencing Practice of the Criminal Court of Philadelphia*, London: Macmillan

—— (1970) 'Race, Social Status and Criminal Arrest', *American Sociological Review, 35*, 476-90

Gubrium, J.F. (1974) 'Victimization in Old Age', *Crime and Delinquency, 20*, 245-50

Hackler, J.C., Ho, K.-Y. and Urquhart-Ross, C. (1974) 'The Willingness to Intervene: Differing Community Characteristics', *Social Problems, 21*, 329-44

Hagan, J. (1974) 'Extra-legal Attributes and Criminal Sentencing: An Assessment of a Sociological Viewpoint', *Law and Society Review,*

8, 357-83

—— (1977) 'Criminal Justice in Rural and Urban Communities: A Study of the Bureaucratization of Justice', *Social Forces, 55*, 597-612

Hall, S., Critcher, C., Jefferson, T., Clarke, J. and Roberts, B. (1978) *Policing the Crisis: Mugging, the State, and Law and Order*, London: Macmillan

Hammond, J.L. (1973) 'Two Sources of Error in Ecological Correlations', *American Sociological Review, 38*, 764-77

Hardt, R.H. and Peterson, S.J. (1968) 'Neighbourhood Status and Delinquency Activity as Indexed by Police Activity and a Self-reported Survey', *Criminologica, 6*, 37-51

Hargreaves, D. (1967) *Social Relations in a Secondary School*, London, Routledge & Kegan Paul

Harries, K.D. (1971) 'The Geography of American Crime, 1968', *Journal of Geography, 70*, 204-13

—— (1974) *The Geography of Crime and Justice*, New York: McGraw-Hill

—— (1975) 'Rejoinder to Richard Peet: "The geography of crime: a political critique" ', *Professional Geographer, 27*, 280-2

—— (1976) 'Observations on Radical Versus Liberal Theories of Crime Causation', *Professional Geographer, 28*, 100-3

—— (1980) *Crime and the Environment* (No. 1035 American Lecture Series), Springfield, Illinois: C.C. Thomas

Harries, K.D. and Brunn, S.D. (1978) *The Geography of Laws and Justice: Spatial Perspectives on the Criminal Justice System*, New York: Praeger

Harries, K.D. and Lura, R.P. (1974) 'The Geography of Justice: Sentencing Variations in U.S. Judicial Districts', *Judicature, 57*, 392-401

Hartnagel, T.F. (1979) 'The Perception and Fear of Crime: Implications for Neighbourhood Cohesion, Social Activity and Community Affect', *Social Forces, 58*, 176-93

Haynes, R.M. (1973) 'Crime Rates and City Size in America', *Area, 5*, 162-5

Herbert, D.T. (1976) 'The Study of Delinquency Areas: A Social Geographical Approach', *Transactions, Institute of British Geographers*, NS *1*, 472-92

—— (1977a) 'An Areal and Ecological Analysis of Delinquency Residence: Cardiff 1966 and 1971', *Tijdschrift voor Economische en Sociale Geografie, 68*, 83-99

—— (1977b) 'Crime, Delinquency and the Urban Environment', *Progress in Human Geography, 1*, 208-39

—— (1979) 'Urban Crime: A Geographical Perspective' in D.T. Herbert and D.M. Smith (eds.), *Social Problems and the City*, London: Oxford University Press, pp. 115-38

Higgins, P.C., Richards, P.J. and Swan, J.H. (1976) 'Crowding and Crime Rates: A Comment', *Urban Affairs Quarterly, 11*, 309-16

Hindelang, M.J. (1976) *Criminal Victimization in Eight American Cities: A Descriptive Analysis of Common Theft and Assault*, Cambridge, Mass.: Ballinger

—— (1978) 'Race and Involvement in Common Law Personal Crimes', *American Sociological Review, 43*, 93-109

Hindelang, M.J., Gottfredson, M.R. and Garofalo, J. (1978) *Victims of Personal Crime: An Empirical Foundation for a Theory of Personal Victimization*, Cambridge, Mass.: Ballinger

Hirschi, T. and Selvin, H.C. (1967) *Delinquency Research*, New York: Free Press

Hogarth, J. (1971) *Sentencing as a Human Process*, Toronto: University of Toronto Press

Home Office (1973) *Shoplifting and Thefts by Shop Staff: Report of a Working-Party on Internal Shop Security*, London: HMSO

—— (1980) *Criminal Statistics, England and Wales, 1979*, Cmnd 8098, London: HMSO

Hood, R.G. (1962) *Sentencing in Magistrates' Courts: A Study in Variation in Policy*, London: Stevens

—— (1972) *Sentencing the Motoring Offender: A Study of Magistrates' Views and Practices*, London: Heinemann

Hood, R.G. and Sparks, R.F. (1970) *Key Issues in Criminology*, London: Weidenfeld & Nicholson

Hough, J.M., Clarke, R.V.G. and Mayhew, P. (1980) 'Introduction' to R.V.G. Clarke and P. Mayhew (eds.), *Designing Out Crime*, London: HMSO, pp. 1-17

Huntington, E. (1945) *Mainsprings of Civilization*, New York: Wiley

Hurley, W. and Monahan, T.M. (1969) 'Arson: The Criminal and the Crime', *British Journal of Criminology, 9*, 4-21

Irving, H.W. (1978) 'Space and Environment in Interpersonal Relations' in D.T. Herbert and R.J. Johnston (eds.), *Geography and the Urban Environment*, Vol. 1, London: Wiley, pp. 249-84

Jacobs, J. (1961) *Death and Life of Great American Cities*, London: Cape

Jeffery, C.R. (1976) 'Criminal Behavior and the Physical Environment',

American Behavioral Scientist, 20, 149-74

Johnstone, J.W.C. (1978) 'Social Class, Social Areas and Delinquency', *Sociology and Social Research, 63*, 49-72

Jones, H. (1958) 'Approaches to an Ecological Study', *British Journal of Delinquency, 8*, 277-93

Kania, R.R.E. and Mackey, W.C. (1977) 'Police Violence as a Function of Community Characteristics', *Criminology, 15*, 27-48

Kettle, M. (1979) 'Running a Tight Court', *New Society*, 1 March

Kitsuse, J.I. and Cicourel, A.V. (1963) 'A Note on the Uses of Official Statistics', *Social Problems, 11*, 131-9

Kleinman, P.H. and David, D.S. (1973) 'Victimization and Perception of Crime in a Ghetto Community', *Criminology, 11*, 307-43

Lambert, J.R. (1970) *Crime, Police and Race Relations*, London: Oxford University Press for the Institute of Race Relations

Lander, B. (1954) *Towards an Understanding of Juvenile Delinquency*, New York: Columbia University Press

Lee, Y., Leung, Y. and Lyles, L. (1974) 'Two Conceptual Approaches and an Empirical Analysis of the Origin Node of Violent Crimes', *Proceedings of the American Association of Geographers, 6*, 157-61

Lemert, E.M. (1967) *Human Deviance, Social Problems and Social Control*, Englewood Cliffs, NJ: Prentice-Hall

Levenson, H. (1980a) 'Outlook Continues Variable: Criminal Legal Aid 1978', *Legal Action Group Bulletin*, January, 7-10

—— (1980b) 'Criminal Legal Aid in Inner London – The True Refusal Rates', *Legal Action Group Bulletin*, April, 82-3

Ley, D. (1975) 'The Street Gang in its Milieu' in G. Gappert and H.M. Rose (eds.), *The Social Economy of Cities*, Beverley Hills: Sage

Ley, D. and Cybriwsky, R. (1974) 'The Spatial Ecology of Stripped Cars', *Environment and Behavior, 6*, 53-68

Lipton, D., Martinson, R. and Wilks, J. (1975) *Effectiveness of Correctional Treatment: a Survey of Evaluation Studies*, New York: Praeger

Loftin, C. and Hill, R.H. (1974) 'Regional Sub-culture and Homicide: An Examination of the Gastil-Hackney Thesis', *American Sociological Review, 39*, 714-24

Lunden, W.A. (1957) *The Courts and Criminal Justice in Iowa*, Ames, Iowa: Iowa State College

McAllister, J. and Mason, A. (1972) 'A Comparison of Juvenile Delinquents and Children in Care: An Analysis of Socio-economic Factors', *British Journal of Criminology, 12*, 280-6

McClintock, F.H. (1963) *Crimes of Violence*, London: Macmillan

McClintock, F.H. and Avison, N.H. (1968) *Crime in England and*

Wales, London: Heinemann

McClintock, F.H. and Gibson, E. (1961) *Robbery in London*, London: Macmillan

McCulloch, J.W., Smith, N.J. and Batta, I.D. (1975) 'A Comparative Study of Adult Crime Among Asians and Their Host Population', *Probation Journal, 21*, 16-21

McDonald, L. (1969) *Social Class and Delinquency*, London: Faber

McPherson, M. (1978) 'Realities and Perceptions of Crime at the Neighbourhood Level', *Victimology, 3*, 319-28

Maccoby, E.E., Johnson, J.P., and Church, R.M. (1958) 'Community Integration and the Social Control of Juvenile Delinquency', *Journal of Social Issues, 38*, 38-51

Mack, J. (1964) 'Full-time Miscreants, Delinquent Neighbourhoods, and Criminal Networks', *British Journal of Sociology, 15*, 38-53

Marx, G.T. and Archer, D. (1971) 'Citizen Involvement in the Law Enforcement Process: The Case of Community Patrols', *American Behavioral Scientist, 15*, 52-72

Marx, G.T. and Archer, D. (1973) 'The Urban Vigilante', *Psychology Today, 6*, 45-50

Matza, D. (1964) *Delinquency and Drift*, New York: Wiley

—— (1969) *Becoming Deviant*, Englewood Cliffs, NJ: Prentice-Hall

Mawby, R.I. (1977a) 'Kiosk Vandalism', *British Journal of Criminology, 17*, 30-46

—— (1977b) 'Defensible Space: A Theoretical and Empirical Appraisal', *Urban Studies, 14*, 169-79

—— (1979a) 'The Victimization of Juveniles: A Comparative Study of Three Areas of Publicly Owned Housing in Sheffield', *Journal of Research in Crime and Delinquency, 16*, 98-113

—— (1979b) *Policing the City*, Farnborough: Saxon House

Mayhew, H. (1864) *London Labour and the London Poor*, four volumes, London: Griffin, Bohn

Mayhew, P. (1979) 'Defensible Space: The Current Status of a Crime Prevention Theory', *Howard Journal, 18*, 150-9

Mayhew, P., Clarke, R.V.G. and Hough, J.M. (1980) 'Steering Column Locks and Car Theft' in R.V.G. Clarke and P. Mayhew (eds.), *Designing Out Crime*, London: HMSO, pp. 19-30

Mercer, C. (1975) *Living in Cities: Psychology and the Urban Environment*, Harmondsworth, Middlesex: Penguin

Merton, R.K. (1957) *Social Theory and Social Structure*, New York: Free Press

Miller, W.B. (1958) 'Lower Class Culture as a Generating Milieu of Gang Delinquency', *Journal of Social Issues, 14*, 5-19

Mizruchi, E.H. and Perrucci, R. (1962) 'Norm Qualities and Differential Effects of Deviant Behavior: An Exploratory Analysis', *American Sociological Review, 27*, 391-9

Mladenka, K.R. and Hill, K.Q. (1976) 'A Reexamination of the Etiology of Urban Crime', *Criminology, 13*, 491-506

Montgomery, P.L. (1973) 'Its Crime Indigenous to Westchester', *The New York Times*, 13 May (quoted in Conklin, 1975, pp. 31-2)

Morris, D. (1969) *The Human Zoo*, London: McGraw-Hill

Morris, T.P. (1957) *The Criminal Area*, London: Routledge & Kegan Paul

Moses, E. (1947) 'Differentials in Crime Rates Between Negroes and Whites based on Comparisons of Four Socio-economically Equated Areas', *American Sociological Review, 12*, 411-20

Mulvihill, D.J. and Tumin, M.M. (1969) *Crimes of Violence,* Vol. 11, National Commission on the Causes and Prevention of Violence, Washington: US Governent Printing Office

National Research Council (1976) *Surveying Crime*, Washington: National Academy of Sciences

Newman, O. (1972) *Defensible Space: People and Design in the Violent City*, London: Architectural Press

—— (1975) *Design Guidelines for Creating Defensible Space*, Washington: US Government Printing Office

Normandeau, A. (1969) 'Robbery in Philadelphia and London', *British Journal of Criminology, 9*, 71-9

Pablant, P. and Baxter, J.C. (1975) 'Environmental Correlates of School Vandalism', *Journal of the American Institute of Planners, 41*, 270-9

Patchett, K.W. and McClean, J.D. (1965) 'Decision-making in Juvenile Cases', *Criminal Law Review*, 699-710

Peach, C. (1975) 'The Spatial Analysis of Ethnicity and Class', Introduction to C. Peach (ed.), *Urban Social Segregation*, London: Longman

Peet, R. (1975) 'The Geography of Crime: A Political Critique', *Professional Geographer, 27*, 277-80

—— (1976) 'Further Comments on the Geography of Crime', *Professional Geographer, 28*, 96-100

Phillips, P.D. (1973) 'Risk-related Crime Rates and Crime Patterns', *Proceedings of the Association of American Geographers, 5*, 221-4

Polk, K. (1957) 'Juvenile Delinquency and Social Areas', *Social Prob-*

lems, 5, 214-17

—— (1967) 'Urban Social Areas and Delinquency', *Social Problems, 14,* 320-5

Pope, C.E. (1975) *Sentencing of California Felony Offenders*, Washington: US Government Printing Office

Poveda, T.G. (1972) 'The Fear of Crime in a Small Town', *Crime and Delinquency, 18,* 147-53

Power, M.J., Benn, R.T. and Morris, J.N. (1972) 'Neighbourhood, School and Juveniles Before the Courts', *British Journal of Criminology, 12,* 111-32

Pyle, G.F. (1974) *The Spatial Dynamics of Crime*, Chicago: University of Chicago, Department of Geography Research Paper No 159

—— (1976a) 'Geographic Perspectives on Crime and the Impact of Anticrime Legislation' in J.S. Adams (ed.), *Urban Policymaking and Metropolitan Dynamics*, Cambridge, Mass.: Ballinger, pp. 257-91

—— (1976b) 'Spatial and Temporal Aspects of Crime in Cleveland, Ohio', *American Behavioral Scientist, 20,* 175-97

Quinney, R. (1964) 'Crime, Delinquency and Social Areas', *Journal of Research in Crime and Delinquency, 1,* 149-54

Radzinowicz, L. (1957) *Sexual Offences*, London: Macmillan

Reiss, A.J. (1971) *Police and Public*, New Haven: Yale University Press

Reiss, A.J. and Rhodes, A.L. (1961) 'The Distribution of Juvenile Delinquency in the Social Class Structure', *American Sociological Review, 26,* 720-32

Reppetto, T.A. (1974) *Residential Crime*, Cambridge, Mass.: Ballinger

—— (1976a) 'Crime Prevention and the Displacement Phenomenon', *Crime and Delinquency, 22,* 166-77

—— (1976b) 'Crime Prevention Through Environmental Policy: A Critique', *American Behavioral Scientist, 20,* 275-88

Rex, J. and Moore, R. (1967) *Race, Community and Conflict*, London: Oxford University Press

Reynolds P.D. (1973) *Victimization in a Metropolitan Region* (mimeo), Minneapolis: University of Minnesota Centre for Sociological Research

Roncek, D.W. (1975) 'Density and Crime: A Methodological Critique', *American Behavioral Scientist, 18,* 843-60

Rossi, P.H., Waite, E., Bose, C. and Berk, R.E. (1974) 'The Seriousness of Crime: Normative Structure and Individual Differences', *American Sociological Review, 39,* 224-37

Rubinstein, J. (1973) *City Police*, New York: Ballantine

Sacks, H. (1972) 'Note on Police Assessment of Moral Character' in

D. Sudnow (ed.), *Studies in Social Interaction*, New York: Free Press

Scarr, H.A. (1973) *Patterns of Burglary*, Washington: US Government Printing Office

Schaffer, E.B. (1980) *Community Policing*, London: Croom Helm

Schmid, C.F. (1960) 'Urban Crime Areas, Parts I and II', *American Sociological Review, 25*, 527-54, 655-78

Schmitt, R.C. (1957) 'Density, Delinquency and Crime in Honolulu', *Sociology and Social Research, 41*, 274-6

—— (1963) 'Implications of Density in Hong Kong', *Journal of the American Institute of Planners, 29*, 210-17

Scott, P. (1972) 'The Spatial Analysis of Crime and Delinquency', *Australian Geographical Studies, 10*, 1-18

Sellin, T. and Wolfgang, M.E. (1964) *The Measurement of Delinquency*, New York: Wiley

Shaw, C.R. (1929) *Delinquency Areas*, Chicago: University of Chicago Press

Shaw, C.R. and McKay, H.D. (1942) *Juvenile Delinquency and Urban Areas*, Chicago: University of Chicago Press (revised edition, 1969)

Skogan, W.G. (1976) 'Crime and Crime Rates' in W.G. Skogan (ed.), *Sample Surveys of the Victims of Crime*, Cambridge, Mass.: Ballinger, pp. 105-19

Smith, D.M. (1974) *Crime Rates as Territorial Social Indicators: the Case of the United States*, London: Queen Mary College Occasional Papers No 1

Smith, T.S. (1976) 'Inverse Distance Variations for the Flow of Crime in Urban Areas', *Social Forces, 54*, 802-15

Sommer, R. (1969) *Personal Space: the Behavioral Basis of Design*, Englewood Cliffs, NJ: Prentice Hall

Sparks, R.F., Genn, H.G. and Dodd, D.J. (1977) *Surveying Victims: A Study of the Measurement of Criminal Victimization, Perceptions of Crime, and Attitudes to Criminal Justice*, Chichester: Wiley

Stephenson, L.K. (1974) 'Spatial Dispersion of Intra-urban Juvenile Delinquency', *Journal of Geography, 73*, 20-6

Stevens, P. and Willis, C.F. (1979) *Race, Crime and Arrests*, Home Office Research Study No 58, London: HMSO

Sturman, A. (1980) 'Damage on Buses: The Effects of Supervision' in R.V.G. Clarke and P. Mayhew (eds.), *Designing Out Crime*, London: HMSO, pp. 31-8

Sundeen, R.A. and Mathieu, J.T. (1976) 'The Urban Elderly: Environments of Fear' in J. Goldsmith and S.S. Goldsmith (eds.), *Crime and the Elderly*, Lexington, Mass.: Lexington Books, pp. 51-66

Sutherland, E.H.(1939) *Principles of Criminology*, 2nd edition, New York: Lippincott

Suttles, G. (1972) *The Social Construction of Communities*, Chicago: University of Chicago Press

Taylor, I., Walton, P. and Young, J. (1973) *The New Criminology: for a Social Theory of Deviance*, London: Routledge & Kegan Paul

—— (1975) 'Critical Criminology in Britain: Review and Prospects' in I. Taylor, P. Walton and J. Young (eds.), *Critical Criminology*, London: Routledge & Kegan Paul, pp. 6-62

Taylor, L. (1973) 'The Meaning of the Environment' in C. Ward (ed.), *Vandalism*, London: Architectural Press, pp. 54-63

Thornberry, T.P. (1973) 'Race, Socio-economic Status and Sentencing in the Juvenile Justice System', *Journal of Criminal Law and Criminology, 64*, 90-8

Thrasher, F. (1927) *The Gang*, Chicago: Chicago University Press

Tulloch, P. (1978) 'Normative Theory and Social Policy', *The Australian and New Zealand Journal of Sociology, 14*, 65-75

Turner, S. (1969) 'Delinquency and Distance' in T. Sellin and M.E. Wolfgang (eds.), *Delinquency: Selected Studies*, New York: Wiley, pp. 11-26

Waller, I. and Okihiro, N. (1978) *Burglary: The Victim and the Public*, Toronto: University of Toronto Press

Wallis, C.P. and Maliphant, R. (1967) 'Delinquent Areas in the County of London: Ecological Factors', *British Journal of Criminology, 7*, 250-84

Walmsley, R. and White, K. (1979) *Sexual Offences, Consent, and Sentencing*, Home Office Research Study No 54, London: HMSO

Walsh, D.P. (1978) *Shoplifting: Controlling a Major Crime*, London: Macmillan

Wheeler, S., Bonacich, E., Cramer, M.R. and Zola, I.K. (1968) 'Agents of Delinquent Control: a Comparative Analysis' in S. Wheeler (ed.), *Controlling Delinquents*, New York: Wiley, pp. 31-60

Wiles, P. (1975) 'Criminal Statistics and Sociological Explanations of Crime' in W.G. Carson and P. Wiles (eds.), *The Sociology of Crime and Delinquency in Britain*, vol. 1, London: Martin Robertson, pp. 198-219

Wilkes, J.A. (1967) 'Ecological Correlates of Crime and Delinquency' in *Task Force Report: Crime and its Impact*, Appendix A, Washington: US Government Printing Office

Willie, C.V. (1967) 'The Relative Contribution of Family Status and

Economic Status to Juvenile Delinquency', *Social Problems, 14*, 326-35

Wilson, J.Q. (1968) *Varieties of Police Behavior*, Cambridge, Mass.: Harvard University Press

Wilson, R. (1963) *Difficult Housing Estates*, London: Tavistock

Winsborough, H.H. (1962) 'City Growth and City Structure', *Journal of Regional Science, 4*, 35-49

Wolf, P. and Hauge, R. (1975) 'Criminal Violence in Three Scandinavian Countries' in *Scandinavian Studies in Criminology*, vol. 5, London: Tavistock

Wolfgang, M.E., Figlio, R.M. and Sellin, T. (1972) *Delinquency in a Birth Cohort*, Chicago: Chicago University Press

Won, G. and Yamamoto, G. (1968) 'Social Structure and Deviant Behavior: a Study of Shoplifting', *Sociology and Social Research, 53*, 44-55

Yablonsky, L. (1962) *The Violent Gang*, Harmondsworth, Middlesex: Penguin

INDEX